D1084187

SAINT JOHN AND THE APOCALYPSE

SAINT JOHN

— AND THE —

APOCALYPSE

C.C. MARTINDALE, S.J.

Roman Catholic Books

Post Office Box 2286, Fort Collins, CO 80522
BooksforCatholics.com

Nihil Obstat:
G.H. Joyce, S.J.,
Censor Deputatus

Imprimatur:
Edm. Can. Surmont,
Vicarius Generalis

Westmonasterii,
Die 7 Decembris, 1922

ISBN 1-929291-79-5

CONTENTS

INTRODUCTION

HERE, no complete commentary is to be expected; recondite theories are not discussed, especially astronomical ones, and several obscure points are left obscure, for St. John often alludes to what might be understood only by his immediate Asiatic environment, and soon ceased to be —or never was—intelligible to men of some other culture, like that of the West. Still, the Apocalypse is an inspired book, forming part of the New Testament. It is true that it may be more generally useful at one moment of the Church's history than at another—say, at the beginning of the Christian era, or towards the close of all history alike— but it can never be useless. The pose of almost cynical amusement taken by some, when they hear that anyone is studying the Apocalypse, appears to be a very sacrilegious impertinence. Its author promises a quite special blessing to those who "read it aloud" and listen to and keep its words. On those who wilfully add to or subtract from them, he pronounces a grave condemnation. Moreover, it has been loved at all times by Catholic saints; it can be read and re-read, with passionate, thrilled interest—I have experienced—by children; and unlimited consolation and encouragement can be drawn by all from its many passages of incomparable beauty, tenderness, and sublimity. It is remarkable how those who speak superficially, if not frivolously, about it, fasten on, as though representative of the whole, precisely those passages which in a sense are least so, or on images which, if at first sight unintelligible or even grotesque, would, after a little trouble, lose all their grotesqueness and reveal much far from recondite significance.

There are, then, certain points, which would all have to be treated fully in a true commentary, on which I hardly touch at all, save most briefly in this introduction.

One is the question of authorship.

I have no doubt that the "John" who so simply places his name at the head of the book—who writes as one having unquestioned and general authority in the Asian Churches—who takes it for granted that his missive will be everywhere read aloud, as he directs, and will be regarded as absolutely intangible and sacrosanct; that this man who writes in Greek while he thinks in Aramaic; whose very diction presents, together with its extraordinary divergences from, such singular alliances with, that of the Fourth Gospel (and the links are precisely those very subtle ones which do more to consolidate a connection than mere obvious coincidences); whose doctrine and, so to call it, spiritual imagination are so profoundly akin to those of the Evangelist—is in fact none other than the author of the Fourth Gospel and of the three Epistles of St. John; that is to say, John, the son of Zebedee, the beloved disciple of Our Lord. And when we add that an early, very widespread, and almost unanimous tradition says the same, and that the divergences in the tradition would never have come about save on account of certain doctrinal preoccupations, we may be sure that we know who the author of the Apocalypse really was.

As for the problem of the language, it certainly is very great; but neither into that do we wish to go in detail. Enough to say that in every superficial way the apocalyptic diction, with its amazing mistakes in sheer Greek grammar and syntax, its violent dislocations, its foreign use of words and constructions, is seemingly as unlike as can be to that of the Fourth Gospel, despite the connecting links that we have mentioned. Hence the difficulty felt by many in ascribing the two documents to the same author. Indeed, not only is the Greek of the Apocalypse unlike that of the Gospel, but unlike any Greek anywhere—at least so far as discoveries permit us as yet to judge. And even allowing for the extraordinary things St. John wanted to say in this book, and the extraordinary condition of soul in which he was while saying them, the problem, we think, remains. It is by no means forbidden to us to surmise that St. John's disciples may have smoothed or improved the Greek of the Gospel without modifying the sense of what its author said; and this hypothesis appeals to us personally, though by no means exclusively. We are most ready to insist that one and the selfsame man may be able to write in very different styles, but he must have some special reason for writing now almost in one language and again in another. And we cannot at present see a cogent reason for St. John's having *chosen* such very different styles in the case of these two books. Père Allo (see below) thinks that John, at "hard labour" in the quarries of Patmos, could only, as it were, jot down quite rough drafts of what he meant to say, and had neither time nor opportunity for polishing them, or even for writing them with that care which he could bestow on the Fourth Gospel, composed at his ease in Ephesus. But John at least had time and opportunity to put the material of the Apocalypse together into the amazingly intricate design in which it as a matter of fact exists; and this, to my thinking, was a far more difficult task than writing rather slowly in good Greek, had he been able to use that. I still think that John in his exile was deprived of that assistance which he could rely on at home, and wrote as he did partly because that was his natural way of writing, and partly because he wrote under the shock, so to say, of so fierce an ecstasy that even such literary graces as he might himself have added were quite out of the question.

The problem of the date at which the Apocalypse was written remains. Tradition is far vaguer on this point. St. Irenæus says definitely that John "saw" the Apocalypse under the Emperor Domitian (d. 96), while in exile at Patmos. Other authorities, however, put that exile under Nero. Others, again, offer dates as early as the reign of Claudius (d. 54), and as late as Trajan (d. 117).

I may mention what has seemed to me as most probable; that John, having written down at quite different periods what may almost be called his "lights in prayer", his visions and his ecstasies, profited by his exile in Patmos—after all, we do not know for certain how he was occupied there, or whether he was actually condemned to hard labour in the quarries—to construct his scattered papers into book form. That something of the sort happened is suggested to me by the way in which, first, he seems to have *all* his material under his eye *from the outset*. He alludes, e.g., to "the" heavenly altar with the definite article, as if it had been already spoken of, though he will not, in fact, utilize it till later; and, again, he has *many* symbolical visions of the *same* thing, which seems to suit a long history of contemplation rather than one continuous ecstasy. It will, too, account for some of the passages of the Apocalypse being far more Jewish in tone than others: his mood may have differed on different occasions, perhaps even according to what he had been reading or talking about, and this may have reflected itself in his way of writing, or in his choice of symbols.

Two points, however, we must make quite clear. There is absolutely nothing in the Apocalypse which even inclines us to think it was not written in its entirety by one man; and we must have no temptation to assign a later rather than an earlier date to it, as though thereby we could avoid certain passages, being sheer predictions, as would be those, for instance, which allude to Emperors who reigned after Nero, had the book been written under Nero. We have no notion, even if we allow the book to have been written at different times, which parts were written first, and we have no desire to hint that prediction plays no part in prophecy.

Having said this, we may sum up by suggesting as probable the idea that the Apocalypse consists of accounts of visions seen, and, perhaps, consigned to writing, at different times, and that they were thus put together by St. John himself during his exile, in the last years of Domitian.

Somewhat similarly I want to say that I have had no intention of making a verse-by-verse interpretation of the Apocalypse's meaning. I certainly repeat that it must have *a* meaning, and that we are right to try to see what it is. But we have very little authoritative Catholic tradition to guide us in any detail. What we can do is this: first, help ourselves by making sure of such historical and material facts as we can; then, consider what the minds of the writer's contemporaries certainly, or probably, had in them and what first they would have discerned in the words they read; and, finally, with all reverence, what St. John's mind may well have had in it as he wrote. When, then, we settle on this or that as the meaning of any passage, we offer it as a probable meaning only for the most part; nor do we dare to say that St. John may not have meant *more* than that; we suggest, throughout, that he probably meant *at least* that. We can hope to reach a probably reliable minimum.

Is this labour lost? Please God, no. It would be so were we to try to tie John's prophecies down to this or that event or person belonging to human history; but there is no limit to the sublimity of the ideas, nor, again, to the practical moral value, as for the government of life, so for the interpretation of the world's history, which are to be derived from his inspired visions, so long as they are not approached at random and arbitrarily.

Students may be referred to the masterpiece of the late Fr. E. B. Allo, O.P., *Apocalypse*, 1921; Fr. R. J. Loenertz, O.P., *The Apocalypse of St. John*, translated by Fr. Hilary Carpenter, O.P., 1947; and other books mentioned in the present writer's article on the Apocalypse in tne *Catholic Commentary on Holy Scripture*.

PART I

THE NATURE AND STRUCTURE OF THE APOCALYPSE

I

PROPHECY AND APOCALYPSE

St. John's Apocalypse seems to define itself. Its title is: *John's Apocalypse, or Revelation*; its first words, "The Revelation of Jesus Christ". And this word "Apocalypse", or "The Removal of the Veil" or "Covering", is not only frequent in the Greek Old Testament, but not rare on the lips of St. Paul. Paul looks for the unveiling of God's righteous judgment (Rom. ii. 5) and for that of the Lord Jesus (1 Cor. i. 7); and all nature yearns for the revealing of the Sons of God (Rom. viii. 19), of that world of supernaturalized humanity, already inaugurated in us, St. John tells, by grace, but not yet made manifest (1 John iii. 2). The mystery which from eternal times had been kept secret is now, through the Spirit, revealed in Christ to the Church (Rom. xvi. 25); to Paul personally "excess" of revelations had been given (2 Cor. xvii. 7); indeed, he holds his Gospel, not from man, nor from human instruction, but from revelation directly made to him by Christ (Gal. i. 12). Even to the faithful, along with other special preternatural gifts, like prophecy, or "speaking with tongues", the graces of spiritual insight, or of interpretation, or of "apocalypse", were, in those early days, freely and mysteriously entrusted.

But St. John's written document can be placed in a more accurate setting; nor, as literature, and speaking widely, is it alone of its kind.

It had always been told that the person and period of the Messiah would be marked by a special outpouring of the Spirit:

I will pour out My Spirit upon all flesh: your sons and your daughters shall prophesy, your old men shall dream dreams, your young men shall see visions; and also upon the servants and the handmaids in those days I will pour out My Spirit. (Joel ii. 28-9.)

St. Peter, quoting this ancient prophecy at Jerusalem, declared that it was then actually being fulfilled (Acts ii. 16ff.); and the same Spirit of Prophecy—the more manifest for its all but unbroken silence of centuries—revealed itself in the passionate preaching of the Baptist; was pre-eminent in Our Lord Himself; followed the footsteps of the Apostles; and swept like a wave over the earliest Church. Indeed, it is significant that in those days, when the theological expression of the dogma of the Third Person in the Most Holy Trinity was so undeveloped, writers like St. Justin will almost exclusively speak of the Holy Spirit in terms of that activity of His which had been so supremely noticeable, and call Him by preference the Spirit of Prophecy.

Nor did prophecy mean, exclusively, prediction of the future. "The witness given by [and to] Jesus is the Spirit of Prophecy." Prediction might certainly be included in prophecy, though in a sense all prophecy was a "witnessing to Christ", and witness given by Christ, truly present by His power before and after, as during, His life on earth. And again, all witnessing to Christ was, in a wide sense, prophecy; all true inspired proclamation, all genuine transcendent encouragement, exhortation, and precept— nay, the most practical advice, political even, is included in the writings of the Prophets. Prophets established and developed, inspired or purified, what Hebrew priests or legislators or kings had begun or forwarded or organized. Even to the work of the Apostles prophets might give analogous service. Not but what, in much of their work, all these—priest, king, or Apostle—might be prophets too; but there was no necessity for a prophet to be anything else save prophet.

Within their number, however, some were to be found who must be called, in a special way, apocalyptists; though, again, their distinguishing mark may almost be said to consist in a greater intensity, or depth, or sublimity of vision, rather than in any quite separate function or spiritual gift, while their intention is scarcely at all—as the Prophets' often is—some practical object to be realized here and now; and they write, for the most part, not only under inspiration, but in ecstasy. No doubt, too, apocalyptists dwelt by preference on the end of all things, and used a language of very specialized symbolism; but ordinary prophets used much allegory, too, of word and act, and perceived spiritual values under, or through, material forms; they, too, dwelt on the ultimate destiny of the people and the world; they, too, had visions unsurpassably sublime.

Perhaps it may be said, not too fancifully, that the habitual gaze of the prophet is focussed on humanity, for the inspired lifting it up to God; that of the apocalyptist upon God, so as to descend thence upon humanity, and to interpret and direct it in terms of that ineffable contemplation. But the prophet might well be granted, at times, the apocalyptist's focus, and in the collected works of such prophets as wrote down what they felt or saw are many "apocalyptic" passages;[1] while in the apocalyptists, and even in St. John, there may be more purely "prophetic" and quite practical elements. And, as we shall see, the

[1] Such are Isa. xiii., xxiv., lxv.; even in the historical or Mosaic books such passages occur: 1 (3) Kings xxii.; Gen. xv. Ezekiel throughout "sets towards" and constantly writes "apocalypse". So, too, often Joel and Zachariah, but it is Daniel who should be reckoned the first example of almost pure apocalypse.

content of both prophet's and apocalyptist's vision might be manifold—for example, an actual or imminent persecution; a general moral truth, such as the conflict of right and wrong; and, the end of the world. All these might be included in one contemplation, and the focus of sight might shift rapidly, as it were, from one depth to another in the perspective.

The special gifts of prophecy and apocalypse diminished rapidly after the first or second Christian generations, and, indeed, were at all times dangerous, difficult to control, exposed to subjectivism and even imitation. But all great Christian saints who have spoken a message to the nations, like St. Bernard or St. Francis Xavier, have a true claim to the name "prophet" in the wider sense, and a Curé d'Ars in the narrower; while St. Peter Damian, and still more St. Vincent Ferrer and some of the women saints, like St. Bridget, can be reckoned as true Christian apocalyptists. And of false prophets there have been legion.

How is the symbolic language, in which apocalyptists expressed their doctrine, to be accounted for? God might, of course, reveal, dictate, the symbols as directly as He might the doctrine. And, of course, the whole message of the apocalyptist (in the case, say, of Daniel, or St. John, or any canonical work) is *inspired*. But it is clear that much of the symbolical language, and even the forms of the language, are traditional and "derived". This is a *literary* origin. Let me, before illustrating that, point out two *psychological* ways in which any writer might come to write under symbolic imagery, whether traditional or not.

Sometimes the spiritual intuition might be so pure and sublime that in no way, save by symbols, could it be suggested to one who had not shared it. The notion might be so tremendous, unaccustomed, impatient of formulæ and phrases, that some other vehicle than definitions for the intellect must be sought. Somewhat thus, Plato, when he felt his scientific statements grown too thin, too skeleton-like in outline for the surpassing glory, on the one hand, and for average intelligence on the other, took refuge in his "myths". Often the seer would himself feel his choice of symbol to be painfully, even ludicrously, inadequate. Perhaps St. John himself felt regretful when certain symbols seemed the traditionally correct material to use. Certainly he *eliminates* much from the material supplied to him by those whom, like Ezekiel, he none the less is following. St. Ignatius, without any doubt, chafed when he had to use the image of three "spinet-keys", separate and yet some-how joined, to describe his vision of the Trinity. Some-times, indeed, the symbolism may be so vague as to be almost as shapeless as that which it is fain to picture, yet significantly so, as in most metaphors drawn by Ezekiel from light. Or, again, it may be almost brutally concrete, a statement of the divine revelation in confessedly alien material, as when he describes God in terms of flashing metals; or when Ignatius says he "saw" Our Lord or Mary, yet denies that he beheld either limb or size or form; or when St. Margaret Mary says she "saw" the Sacred Heart, and then describes it as a crystal globe or a sun. Again and again ecstatics, who constantly use the words "to see", "to hear", and describe forthwith sights and sounds, deny that eye or ear perceived anything whatso-ever. The intuition has to clothe itself in thoughts, and these cannot emerge into the reflex consciousness without *some* robe of imagery, supplied by the imagination, and in the long run through the senses. This is always so when they are to be stated in words.

Now it is observation, or reading, which supplies us with such images and words, the material for symbolism; and though it is true that an active mind can recast, rearrange, group them, yet it cannot quite disregard them, even at its most inventive. Very likely, too, the nucleus of the image, the substantial point where the analogy holds good, may be quite small and simple. The poetic fancy may proceed to develop or decorate this after the revealing light has passed, or at least in its after-glow. So, too, may deliberate reflection. The saints often warn us not to confuse what, in such circumstances, we picture to ourselves with what the divine light really showed us.[1]

Such, then, is the psychological process when a man *first* experiences, whether by natural flash of intuition or by divine revelation, some abstract or spiritual fact, and then seeks to express it in terms of the imagination and then in words.

Quite opposite is the process when a man first perceives some natural object or even idea, and then, in the flash of intuition, or inspired, sees how it stands for or symbolizes or contains an ulterior or spiritual fact. The connection may indeed be quite slight and superficial. May not this have been what happened when the sheer assonance of words proved the link between what was seen and what was ultimately thought, as when Jeremiah sees an almond branch—the Hebrew word for that is *shaked*—and is thus reminded that Yahweh "will watch" (*shoked*) over His word to perform it (Jer. i. 12). Amos, seeing a basket (*kayitz*) of fruit, finds flashing into his mind the assurance that "the end (*ketz*) is come upon My people". The ἀφορμή, the send-off, would here then have been a thing

---

[1] It is equally true, as I said, that reflection can simplify a large and elaborate image which memory had inherited and retains. John quite "dehumanizes" Ezekiel's concrete image of the Eternal God. It is interesting to watch the Hebrews, whose whole duty it was to do without religious imagery as far as might be, continually yielding to their artistic imagination. So, too, St. John of the Cross, whose whole theory tended to the rejection of "images", yields in his lyrics to an unequalled beauty of constructive, pictorial, and sensuous imagination.

seen of which the name sounds like a word which for the Prophet has a religious significance, and God, using this machinery through which to work, strikes from the man a prophetic idea and cry. But when Jeremiah again notices (i. 13) a "seething caldron", he quite naturally sees symbolized in it the imminent turmoil of the nations that so preoccupies him; then, joining itself to his first perception, comes the detail that the caldron fronts from the north; this reinforces and perhaps makes explicit the idea—latent, doubtless, already in the mind of a man strongly concerned even by natural bent with political happenings, present or probable—that the trouble is destined to break out from the great Northern Empire. Again God uses this as the material that He will inspire.[1]

It is this divine inspiration, of which we are guaranteed independently, that turns what else were a mere intuition into a prophecy. There were crowds of contemporary "false prophets", religious politicians quite capable of making shrewd surmises about the future, and who thought and talked of things in much the same way; their psychological processes, so far as their sheer mechanism was concerned, need have differed in no way from those of the inspired prophet, nor is there any rationalism in trying to follow out the way in which that mechanism worked. St. Teresa and St. John of the Cross, and any student of mysticism, constantly do it. What we *know* by divine guarantee, but only thus (though we might independently *surmise* it), is that God Himself puts an electric spark, as it were, into that mechanism, sets it in motion, or at least uses it when it has been in any, even human, way set moving—either uses the natural sight of the "branch" or the "basket", and even the thoughts to which the sight gives

[1] I have not, of course, the hardihood to assert that this *was* the "psychological machinery" of inspiration here, but it *could* have been.

rise, as the material into which to put the soul of inspiration, or causes the sight to suggest those thoughts, or, finally, directly causes the prophet to look at and notice the natural object. In a word, it is more likely God will use the psychical equipment of the man He made than totally supersede it. It is a Catholic principle that grace attends on nature: *gratia sequitur naturam*; and just as our whole works are "grace-works", supernatural, so we must keep it clear that whatever the human mechanism, the natural coefficient, in an inspired seer, he is to be said, quite roundly, to have had *supernatural visions*. It must throughout this book be recalled that not only was St. John *inspired* to write his visions down, but that the visions were supernatural in themselves.

Again, not only direct vision of an object, but memory of any experience, may serve as the starting-point. Such memories a man of powerful spiritual imagination may lay hold of, and (always, in the case of the prophet, under inspiration) forcefully remodel them to suit a higher end. This is less spontaneous, usually, but can be richer in results. Thus, undoubtedly, Ezekiel made use—with more or less deliberation, that we cannot judge of—of those colossal monsters, human-headed, winged, lion- or bull-bodied, which he saw when in captivity in Babylon. Strongly coloured by these are his descriptions of those strange creatures that support God's throne; and again, the throne itself is an indefinitely glorified version of some earthly piece of craftsmanship. Something in this way, St. Aloysius, who had no really creative imagination, laboriously adapted the whole of a ducal court and its etiquette to portray the angelic service of heaven.

The use made by Ezekiel of the Babylonian beasts is reflected in that made by St. John of Ezekiel's strange creations in their turn. For such imagery as forcibly struck popular imagination, after it had been used by some famous seer, tended rapidly to fix itself and become traditional. Symbols repeated themselves again and again across the generations. Poet after poet, artist after artist, re-used the ancient forms, dear to the national feeling and consecrated now by religion. The influence of Daniel on apocalypses properly so-called was enormous. But on the lips of lesser men these forms of speech naturally grew to seem glib or hackneyed, or to be misapplied. A genius would re-soul them with his own spiritual power. Such a genius was St. John. He left nothing of the apocalyptic imagery just as he found it, and almost everything he used he immeasurably improved. Yet even a genius is not all the time at the crest of his inspiration-wave; the impulse may flag; and then, even as he writes, he does so laboriously and will cease so communicatively to express all that he has within him; it may, indeed, in its full significance, be latent to himself. Even a poet scarcely realizes all his meaning; and a prophet need not know, either, the full bearing of his words.

There are here principles that make it much safer for us to study the symbolism of St. John. We need scarcely ever find ourselves left to *mere* conjecture. Sometimes we cannot tell what he means; we may seldom feel sure we know all that he means; but we can always have good reason for relying that we are on the right track and not yielding to arbitrary, subjective fancy.

We see first that he could use much traditional symbolism that was meaningful to a Jew, or to a Judaic convert, of his period, but that need not appeal to us, alien in blood and distant in time and space. We need not feel half impious if imagery dear to their minds cannot be of value to ours. Even the meaning of details may be quite lost to us, and for ever, having never been anything save locally applicable, and understood not even by men of the ensuing generation, or non-Asiatics. Indeed, we may think that the fact that the book was known to be by John sufficed to carry it far abroad; but again, that the book was precisely *this* book, and half-unintelligible to a Gaulish or even a Roman Christian, would make it looked on with discomfort, embarrassment, and might even end by throwing doubts upon its authorship.

Further, we are made alert to distinguish the substance of the symbol from its decoration or elaboration, to discern the only vital point of contact, and not to waste time trying to evolve an interpretation for each detail of a picture, seeing that they are there only to make it vivid and to "carry it across". Not even in the parables ought we to expect to find an equal amount of doctrinal applicability in each detail of the story.

Again, we are invited to expect that in some cases the sight of a material object will have come first—for example, a volcano, a meteor, a waterfall—and then the material event or fact may be half deserted for the sake of the spiritual thing suggested by it. In other cases, some overwhelming spiritual concept will have come first—for example, the Holy Trinity, or the presence of Christ in the Church—and then the image may be offered almost under protest, as the poor, yet best, algebraic formula, almost, of what it seeks to convey.

And we should add that these two sorts of symbols unite at least in this—they are there to reveal, each in its measure, the hidden. But another kind exists, not to reveal, but to conceal. It is chosen, not by poetic preference, nor in helpless ecstasy, but because it would have been dangerous to speak plainly. Much, if not most, apocalypse was written to encourage the faithful during, or on the eve of, persecution. Thus the latter part of Daniel clearly envisages the period of Antiochus Epiphanes; and John's Apocalypse alludes to the reigns of Domitian and Nero, and to the Asiatic troubles generally. The Christian community would have been worse endangered should its literature be seen to attack the Government or to preach "disloyalty". Thus certain parts of such apocalypses would be written, quite deliberately, "in cipher". And other things were too holy to be alluded to save under veils, as, for example, the Eucharist.

We shall, then, remember that some of an apocalypse will probably deal directly and primarily with historical facts, some with a spiritual truth. So it were futile to try to interpret such a document as, in all its parts equally, history disguised; or, again, to refuse to look for any interest in historical facts on the part of its writer. No one key will open all its locks. A reader will, then, be wise to start, when possible, from ascertainable elements, such as the conditions of the apocalyptist's times and environment; the necessary, or probable, contents of his memory; the normally probable or possible limits of his self-expression; and then only go on to seek for transcendental meanings. Yet he should also be careful to remember that the seer is never dealing with human happenings merely for their own sake.

Shall we say that there are, or may be, quite five levels in an apocalyptist's consciousness?

He can see concrete facts—e.g., this or that emperor—and may deal with them directly, though sometimes in cipher. (He sees them, however, under the light of morality, or worship; in connection with religion.)

He may see them, too, as typical; thus, not merely one war, or persecution, or martyrdom, or city; but a universal and world-long struggle between opposing ideas, or an undying witness, or materialist civilization as a whole.

He may then also see, in man's soul, or in the world at

large, supernatural influences, tendencies, triumphs, defeats and transmutations.

And, shifting still further his perspective, he may contemplate a world composed of the spiritual prototypes, the truer realities of all these shadowy, transitory, departmental things, an "ideal" world.

Finally—and here, perhaps, he is his truest self—he will contemplate God Himself, and descend thence, with troubled wing and anxious eye, towards humanity; or, again, rest singing his wild yet solemn hymn of ecstasy, eye fixed on the divine.

It were a matter of preternatural delicacy, and yet audacity, to try thus to diagnose and evaluate the psychic level of a prophet's consciousness on each occasion, especially as he may pass rapidly from one to the other and back again, or even may be "seeing" more than one perspective at a time.[1] Enough to have formulated some principles for scanning evidence, some hints towards the formation of a judgment; to provide some hope at least of seeing through John's eyes, of hearing with the ears of those to whom his book was for the first time read. The rest we must leave to the guidance of God's Spirit and to the permissions of the Church. For, once more, we shall never forget that whether we be right or wrong in our views on the human coefficient, the human psychological machinery, we are certain about the divine coefficient, the guaranteed inspiration. However wholly an inspired book is its human author's book, it is also wholly that of its divine Author. In a line—*John's* words have *God* for Author.

[1] A crude illustration: Stand in front of a plate-glass window. You can usually see either what is behind the glass or the reflections upon it. With a little effort you can see the two at the same time—e.g., the image of yourself and the objects displayed beyond, and even the reflection of the street behind you. And all the while you may be *thinking* of the price of a dress, of national economic conditions and general social history. But it is difficult to keep all this equally in your eye or in your mind.

Not all prophets wrote down what they said, and, doubtless, not all apocalyptists what they saw. Yet a certain number of apocalypses, Jewish, Christian, and mixed, have survived besides St. John's. The most important, save, of course, Daniel's, which is a canonical book and inspired, is the Book of Enoch, supposed to be compiled of fragments written at various dates between 166 and 64 B.C. With its name may be associated the Book of the Secrets of Enoch, perhaps A.D. 1-50; both of these contain much imagery which is used by St. John too, such as the Tree of Life;[1] angels, of course, figure largely in them, as indeed they do, with increasing frequency, in Jewish literature, from the Persian Captivity onwards. But the Apocalypse of Baruch, later, it is thought, than the fall of Jerusalem (70), is in many ways yet closer to St. John's. The fall of Rome, and the New Jerusalem, millenarian expectations which excited even Christians, and references to the Messianic triumph which, St. Irenæus says, were even thought to have originated with Christ Himself, are noticeable in it. Finally, the Fourth Book of Esdras, probably written under Domitian, and therefore contemporary, it seems likely, with the completed form of the Apocalypse, is planned out—at least, in the part that concerns us—into seven visions. It is on the whole pessimistic, though ruined Jerusalem is to be restored, Messiah is to come, and Rome, under the figure of an eagle, is judged by the Messiah, under the figure of a lion. Of other Jewish books, like the Assumption of Moses, the Ascension of Isaiah, the Apocalypses of Adam, of Elijah, and of Zephaniah; the Testaments of the Twelve Patriarchs and the Sibylline Oracles (Jewish and Christian), the last-named has perhaps most points of contact with St. John's work, though I do not mean by saying that to

---

[1] Some material may be called, even, the "commonplace" of apocalypse —falling stars, earthquakes, eagles, lions, trumpets, and certain *numbers*.

suggest that he had so much as read these books—very dull, on the whole, exaggerated and artificial—still less, that he quotes or even uses them. Some, indeed, or most, are posterior to him. The same literary dialect is, to a varying degree, used in all of them: that is all. Some Christian (or gnostic) apocalypses are known, like the *Anabaticon Pauli* and the Apocalypse of Peter, of which a large fragment survives, was once highly thought of, and made a good fight to get into the canon; on the other hand, St. John's Apocalypse here and there shared the suspicion which finally grew too strong for that of Peter. The fourth-century Apocalypse of Paul is stigmatized by Augustine as no less silly than presumptuous in its claim to narrate the "secret words" heard by St. Paul in ecstasy (2 Cor. xii. 4); and the Greek Apocalypse of St. John relates the further visions of that Apostle on Mount Tabor. Apart from the apocalyptic passages in the Gospels, and those in St. Jude's and St. Peter's Epistles, there is no canonical New Testament apocalypse save St. John's.

These names, however, have been mentioned to make it clear that John's work, though unique in inspirational dignity and spiritual character, and, indeed, in sheer literary value, was not, in its literary character, an isolated phenomenon; it takes its place in a stream of literature flowing across whole centuries. Notice, however, that John's book was the first to bear, explicitly, the name *apocalypse*. Other documents either imitated this or have been so named by critics who saw that they were of the same literary *genre* as St. John's. I need spend no time over pagan "apocalypses", like the Hermetic writings, which offered, in Græco-Egyptian circles and elsewhere, pictures of the other world and the like. At least they show how preoccupied people then were with such problems, and that St. John's Apocalypse would have found a sympathetic audience.

While, then, it is clear that John's mind was soaked with the works of the great men we have mentioned, especially Daniel, Ezekiel, and Zechariah, we cannot say that he ever used, consciously or at all, any of the other apocalypses that were circulating in his time. The most we can say is that he was absolutely at home in the apocalyptic atmosphere, and was so familiar with its special phraseology and favourite symbolism that he used these naturally and by preference, and could count on being understood, temperamentally and in the mass, if not in each detail, by his immediate readers. Besides, as I said above, quite apart from his sheer artistry—for, despite what a Greek-formed taste would consider his imperfections, the other apocalypses as sheer literature come nowhere near John's —his tremendous personality would anyhow recast what he borrowed; he scarcely ever quotes, save where the ancient phrasing was so perfect that any substantial alteration would have seemed sacrilege, or when (apparently) he introduces, as St. Paul does, fragments of Christian hymns already dear to Christian feeling. Even so, he rather explicitly alludes to what his readers knew so well than reproduces it. At the outset he stamps his personality on the work by prefixing to it his own name and whereabouts, and speaks clearly to men who knew and had had dealings with him, unlike the other apocalyptists, who took the names of ancient seers and saints—Enoch, Baruch—and threw their compositions back into a half-mythical past. Besides, the contents and inspiration of St. John's Apocalypse are sundered from those of all the rest by the gulf which, when all is said, separates Christianity from the purest, even, of prophetic Judaism; he puts the ancient words to the service of a quite new doctrine, and to my feeling it is almost an offence to compare his glorious book to anything else whatsoever.

II

THE STRUCTURE OF THE APOCALYPSE

JOHN was commanded by God to write down the visions he had seen, and in obedience to this he composed the Book of the Apocalypse. He did this according to a singular and complicated plan, to which he adheres very closely. I shall try to set forth this plan, but no more than sufficiently, leaving out some of its minor articulations. Thus I shall not point out, save here and there, how John dovetails his visions, inserting part of a following theme into that which he is actually relating, or, if you will, causing a section of the actual symbolic narrative to look forward to the next. This would take up too much room, fascinating as it is to work it out.

May the following scheme, then, be regarded as somewhat simplified, for the sake of brevity and clearness.

The book falls into four main parts:

(1) i.-i. 8. A brief general prologue; title, authorship, sanction of the whole work; salutation of its destined recipients, and ascription of praise to Christ.

(2) i. 9-iii. 22. This itself falls into two parts: an inaugural vision of Christ, who commands John to write to the Seven Churches of Asia, telling them "things present and future"; and a sevenfold covering letter to these Seven Churches, in which the "things present"—that is, their actual state—are chiefly insisted on.

(3) iv. 1-xxii. 5. The bulk of the book, dealing with "things future" for the most part, "or ideal".

(4) The epilogue, xxii. 6 to the end.

The bulk of the book is itself, however, constructed on

an exact and singular scheme. It falls into two clear parts—Part A, iv.-xi. and Part B, xii.-xxii. 5. From Part B may indeed be detached xvii. 1-xxii. 5, and I shall call it Part B2.

The articulation of Part A is as follows:

I. (i) *A double preparatory vision:*

(*a*) The eternal worship of God in heaven (iv).

(*b*) The role of God Incarnate, suffering, and triumphant, in universal history (v).

This spectacle remains as an unchanged background, and in front of it are displayed visions of—

I. (ii) *The breaking of seven seals:*

(*a*) A group of *four seals*—four visions of horsemen (vi. 1-6).

(*b*) A group of *two seals*—the cry of the martyrs and the answer to it (vi. 7-17).

(*c*) A *double vision* (vii).

(*d*) The *seventh seal* (viii. 1).

All this is, as it were, the enduring tendency, the other-world preparation, the symbolized idea, of the actual fact, the this-world execution, the symbolized event, shown in II.

II. (i) *A double preparatory vision:*

(*a*) The prayer of the martyrs in heaven (viii. 2-4).

(*b*) Its effects on earth, seen generally (viii. 5).

This, again, remains as a sort of permanent background, and in front of it you see

II. (ii) *The sounding of seven trumpets:*

(*a*) A group of *four trumpets*—four visions of disasters in the realm of inanimate nature (viii. 6-13).

(*b*) A group of *two trumpets*—a double war of spirits and of men (ix).

(*c*) A *double vision* (x., xi. 1-14).

(*d*) The *seventh trumpet* (xi. 15-18).

The articulation of Part B1 is as follows:
A *prefatorial vision* (xi. 19).

I. (i) *A double preparatory vision:*

(*a*) The Woman, Mother of Christ (xii. 1-2).

(*b*) The Dragon, enemy and would-be conqueror of Christ (3-18).

This remains as a general truth behind the historical truths that follow.

I. (ii) *Seven great "mysteries":*

(*a*) A group of *four "mysteries"*—the Dragon, the Wild Beast from the Sea, the Wild Beast from the Land, and the Lamb (xii. 18-xiv. 5).

(*b*) A group of *two "mysteries"* (xiv. 6-13).

(*c*) A *double vision* (xiv. 14-20).

(*d*) The *seventh "mystery"* (xv. 1-4).

II. (i) A *double prefatory vision* (xv. 5-7); then,

II. (ii) *The outpouring of seven bowls—seven plagues:*

(*a*) A group of *four plagues* (xvi. 1-9).

(*b*) A group of *two plagues* (10-12).

(*c*) A *double vision* (13-16).

(*d*) The *seventh plague* (17-21).

PART B2

The articulation of this last part is perhaps not quite so clear. The tremendous emotion under which John writes it, on the other hand, escapes no one, and it may well account for a relative inattention to the mere arrangement of parts.

All the same, I think the usual divisions are by no means disregarded, though they cannot be shown as "plagues", "trumpets", and the like. I suggest, then, the following actual division with more diffidence than the former ones.

I. *A double prefatory vision:*

(*a*) The World-Harlot.

(*b*) The interpretation of this symbol (xvii).

II. *Seven Visions:*

(*a*) A group of *four visions*—the doom of Rome, and the call to the elect to come forth from her (xviii. 1-8); the dirge of Rome (9-20); the destruction of Rome (21-4); the triumph of the Bride of the Lamb, the New Jerusalem (xix. 1-10).

(Or the Dirge may be joined to the foregoing vision, and the vision of the triumphant heavens may be separated from the announcement of the Marriage of the Lamb).

(*b*) A group of *two visions*—the coming forth of Christ as Conqueror (xix. 11-16); the destruction of the Beast (17-21).

(*c*) A *double vision* interposed—the binding of the Dragon and the reign of the Saints for a thousand years (xx. 1-6); the destruction of the Dragon (7-10).

(*d*) A *seventh vision*—the judgment and consummation (11-15).

This is followed by the double vision of God proclaiming the New Jerusalem, and the New Jerusalem itself, corresponding to the double prefatory vision of God and of the Lamb, prefixed to the whole central part of the book (xxi. 1-8; xxi. 9-xxii. 5).

This seems to be all the more likely as an intended arrangement, since the imagery of St. John and his phrasing revert in many ways to those of the very beginning of the Apocalypse, and denote not only unity of authorship, but that the visions have swung full cycle, and that their end is with their origin.

Finally the epilogue, as said above, corresponding to the prologue with its sanction. The authorship and character of the book are reasserted, and the declaration of the responsibility incumbent on its readers.

Even before detailed examination this strange scheme makes it clear that the apocalyptic episodes are placed in a literary and symbolical series, not a historical one. Interpreters have tortured themselves—and the text—in order to find a system even of world's-end history into which all the visions should fit, consecutively, and in that order. Indescribable confusion results from any attempt to cut up history into groups corresponding to the seals, then the trumpets, the bowls, and so on. Nor can we say it is all to happen, just like that, quite at the end. For some of the events relate to contemporary events, or to what is to happen "soon". St. John then uses symbol after symbol to represent, sometimes events, sometimes ideas, and often the same events and ideas. He contemplates the contents of those different planes of consciousness, sometimes together and sometimes singly, and may use the same symbol to describe what he sees now on this, now on that; and again, may use different symbols for the same subject contemplated on one plane only.

We repeat, what strikes us first about the arrangement of the Apocalypse is, precisely, its symmetrical pattern; and if we care to think that John was thus arranging visions seen at very different times, we are at one stroke emancipated from those who try to prove that the book was written by different people—for John's mood and the contents of his pictorial imagination may have changed often and completely in the course of years—and from difficulties arising from a determination to assign it all to one date.

There is, no doubt, a progression in the book, but it is rather one of doctrine, or of depth of understanding a profound—indeed, an inexhaustible—truth, than of mere time.

All this will be clearer as we go forward.

III

THE RECIPIENTS OF THE APOCALYPSE

THE Apocalypse was addressed, in general intent, to the Christian communities of Proconsular Asia, and directly to seven of its cities.

In apocalyptic symbolism, in which numbers stood for much, the number seven stood for completeness, and here the Seven Churches stand for the whole "Church in Asia".[1] Why are these seven communities chosen? Because, it has been suggested, they stood in order on the "great circular road which bound together the most populous, wealthy, and influential part of the province"; they dominated districts, and thence lesser roads radiated to outlying regions with other important cities and churches.

In Asia the Church had been, if not actually planted, vigorously developed by St. Paul's stay of over two years in its chief city, Ephesus. He settled there about 52 or 53, and used to lecture for several hours daily in one of the city schools after the ordinary day's work was done. He left after the great riot of 55, when his attack on the local cult of the Asiatic goddess roused the silver trade against him. Gradually, however, he got in touch with the whole of western Asia, and his letter to the Ephesians was probably a sort of encyclical for all the Asiatic Churches. St. Peter wrote another, making use of St. Paul's; and if, in Paul's two letters to Timothy, it is clear that the Christians' fervour had considerably cooled, from St. Peter's we see

[1] Seven is thus quite normally used in the Old Testament, and in apocalypse especially since Daniel. Philo of Alexandria works out the theory of this significance; and it has been seen that St John's Apocalypse is wholly built up of sevens, or heptads.

that, though not yet officially persecuted, they were soci-
ally disliked, and exposed to continuous discomfort and
probable attack. By the time St. John wrote, indeed, their
state was in many ways very unsatisfactory: even the
orthodox had slackened; there were nascent heresies to
weaken the Church from within; a fierce antagonism of the
Jews beset it from without; and, above all, a life-and-death
struggle could by then be felt to exist between the two great
forces and ideals—Church and Empire—the Lord Jesus
and the Lord Cæsar, the Lamb and the Wild Beast, the
Spouse of Christ and the Harlot, Christ and Anti-Christ;
it was only a matter of time for this to manifest itself
fully.

In 68 the persecutor Nero died, but his cruelties had
impressed the Christian imagination to an extent beyond
our power to exaggerate. During his reign Peter and Paul
had felt able to implore the faithful still to be loyal, and
could recognize that, not in theory alone, but in the concrete, it was still open to a true Christian to stand firm both
by Cæsar and by Christ. But Peter and Paul had both been
killed by Nero. The unimaginative Vespasian (69-79) probably disliked the Jewish-Christian recalcitrants, but was
too easy-going to rank as a savage persecutor. Domitian,
however (81-96), undoubtedly filled that role, in person or
by proxy; for though any anti-Christian activity of his in
Rome itself was swamped, as it were, in the appalling
general butcheries of his last years, yet his devotion to his
own divinity would have stimulated any official who
wished to flatter him to be fierce, especially against those
who refused that worship. In Asia Cæsar-worship dawned
early, developed fast, and was very enthusiastic. City after
city built its temple, or even temples, to the Emperor; and
a league existed whose president, the Asiarch, directed the
worship of the Augusti. Into every department of life—

military, social, commercial—that worship insinuated it-self. To refuse it seemed equivalent to suicide; no career was left open; abstinence, even, seemed to be a supreme declaration against every kind of loyalty and social solidarity. But of this worship more details will be given when we reach the second part of the Apocalypse, where it is always to the front.

With this amount of preparation we can proceed to the book itself. May we neither add to nor wilfully subtract from its words.

PART II

THE APOCALYPSE OF ST. JOHN

I

THE SALUTATION AND THE MANDATORY VISION

JOHN begins by saying clearly what his book will be. It is "The Revelation of Jesus Christ"—Jesus Christ revealing and revealed. To His Son God gave it: the Son transmits it to His servant; he in his turn must hand it on, with all its teaching on "things present and things soon to be"; and blessed was he who should "read it aloud", and blessed they who should "keep" and ponder and apply its words. For the crisis neared (i. 1-3).

> John to the Seven Churches that are in Asia:
> Grace to you and peace
> From Him [that is named]—
> HE WAS, HE IS, AND HE IS TO COME.
> And from
> THE SEVEN SPIRITS
> That are before the throne of God,
> and from
> JESUS CHRIST,
> The faithful Witness, the First-born from the dead,
> The Lord of the kings of the earth.
> To Him who loves us
> And did free us from our sins at the price of His blood—
> Yea, and made of us a kingdom,
> Priests to God His Father—
> To Him
> The glory and the might unto the ages of the ages.
> Amen.

"See, He is coming with the clouds, and Him shall every eye behold; yea, all they that did pierce Him; and because of Him shall all the tribes of the earth beat their breast."

Yea! Amen.
I am the Alpha and the Omega,
Saith the Lord God,
WHO AM, and WHO WAS, and WHO IS TO COME,
The All-Governor (i. 4-8).[1]

After this cry of praise, John places the great vision in which he received his mandate to write. Somewhat so, the three prophets, Isaiah, Jeremiah, Ezekiel, had sheltered their words beneath the heavenly guarantee (Isa. vi.; Jer. i.; Ezek. i.).

This "brother and partner" of those who suffered and endured for Jesus was, in the prison-island of Patmos,

---

[1] Though this is not, as I said, a commentary, it may save confusion if I say at once that the seven spirits are here not angels, not even the seven angels whom late Jewish tradition placed immediately before God's Throne, but the Holy Spirit operative in His sevenfold way, or perhaps upon the Seven Churches. This conception, strange to us, was not strange to those who would recall the "seven eyes of Yahweh that move throughout the earth" (Zech. iv. 10, and cf. below, "the seven eyes of the Lamb", v. 6), and would indicate to them the unity yet diversity of God's action. I think the intention of the verses is definitely Trinitarian, though it was a Jewish habit to associate, as I said, very closely, the seven great angels with the eternal God, and Justin puts the "army of angels" after the Son and before the Holy Spirit, in *1 Apol.* i. 6. And the seven angels will certainly appear further on in the Apocalypse. Stranger, though, from the point of view of language, is John's method of forming the name of God. In this book I cannot quote much Greek; but I will here set down the shape in which "from Him who is", etc., appears in that language: Ἀπὸ ὁ ὢν καὶ ὁ ἦν καὶ ὁ ἐρχόμενος. As a matter of fact, neither Greek, nor perhaps any language, is adequate to express that absolute existence of God which includes what is for us past, present, and future. Literally translated, John's phrase is "the Was, the Being, and the Coming". *Coming*, not "the Will-be", because of the *Parousia*, the final manifestation of God at the Last Day. A nominative, ὁ μάρτυς ὁ πιστός follows directly on χριστοῦ, the genitive. Still stranger departures from normal grammar occur later on. By no means will one explanation account for all alike. They are sometimes due to the difficulty of writing in Greek what you are thinking in Hebrew, or to sheer distraction from the grammar in favour of the absorbing subject; or perhaps, as in the second instance given above, they are exclamatory parentheses. In verse 7 John is combining Dan. vii. 13 with Zach. xii. 10; and cf. his Gospel, xix. 37. Alpha and Omega (cf. xxi. 6, xxii. 13), the Beginning and the End, the First and the Last, are themselves the first and the last letters of the Greek alphabet. The remaining letters are considered as included. God reaches "from end to end".

"rapt in the Spirit on the Lord's day". He hears a voice,
terrible as a trumpet's, bidding him write what he shall see
and send the scroll to the Seven Churches that are in Asia.
He turns to look, and behold, a vision of seven golden
lampstands, and moving about among them a Man,
clothed in a long white priestly robe, and girt with the
royal golden girdle.

> "His head and His hair were white, like wool as white as
> snow; and His eyes, like a flame of fire; and His feet, like
> brass fired in a furnace; and His voice, like the voice of
> many waters."

In His hand He held seven stars; from His mouth came
flashing a two-edged sword; His face shone like the sun in
his strength. John falls prostrate like one dead, but the
Vision touches him and bids him not to fear.

> I am the First and the Last,
> The living One, and dead did I become;
> And behold
> Alive am I, to the ages of the ages,
> And I hold the keys of death and of hell.
> Write then what thou didst see,
> Both things that are, and what shall be thereafter—
> The meaning of the seven stars that thou sawest on My
> right hand,
> And of the seven golden lamps.
> For the seven stars are the angels of the seven Churches,
> And the seven lamps are the seven Churches (i. 17-20).

Here, then, moving about among His Christians, is
Christ, Immortal Life, Master of Death, grasping in His
hand alike the world of heaven and the Church on earth.
And to the Jewish reader would at once be clear what, to
our unaccustomed eye, may be latent—the terrible daring

of St. John, by which, in this passage, redolent in every phrase of the Old Testament, the symbols which that Old Testament had consecrated exclusively to the eternal God are transferred to the risen Jesus. In Daniel's vision the Man who imaged the chosen people and its King is brought to the Ancient of Days, "whose raiment was white like snow, and the hair of His head like pure wool, and His throne was fiery flames" (vii). Albeit in another vision it was but an angel, or possibly God's supreme Messenger, Messiah, whom Daniel saw, with face like lightning and with eyes like lamps of fire, and with limbs flashing like burnished bronze, and the voice of His words like the voice of a multitude, and in His presence, too, the prophet fainted (x. 8, 19); yet assuredly to hold the stars (Job xxxviii. 31) and the keys of the gates of death was, Rabbinic lore knew well, the unshared prerogative of Yahweh. And the "Origin and End" is none but the very God.[1]

But John on his side knew, and in his Gospel was insistently to tell, that all that the Father has and is He pours into the Son—"All Mine are Thine, and Thine Mine"; the Father has put all things into His hand. In Christ, then, the Father is, the very source of life and life itself; and among the faithful and in them the life moves, and to them it gives itself.[2]

---

[1] All the more remarkable is the promise in St. Matt. xvi. 19, both in what it implies about Our Lord, and what it implies about St. Peter.

[2] By no means here only in the New Testament are titles or symbols reserved by Judaism to the Father transferred to the Son. "The Lord" became Christ's characteristic name, like Adonai, "My Lord", for Yahweh; and "those who call upon His Name" is far more rarely spoken, in the New Testament, of the Father's worshippers than of the Son's. Prophecies which of old could have been understood exclusively of Yahweh—like Isa. xl. 3-13, xlviii. 12, 13; Ps. ci. 26-28—are now applied to Jesus; the coming of Christ, in 2 Thess. i. 7, is described in terms once used for that of Yahweh; and in fine those doxologies, or ascriptions of praise, of which the language was once confined to the worship of the only God,

Nor are the apocalyptic visions of Daniel, Isaiah, and Ezekiel the only ones to be thus transcended by St. John, but even the latest, most developed documents of Judaism. The Book of Enoch (xlvi. 14 sqq.) writes that the seer beheld "One who had a head of days, and His head was white like wool", and with Him was another, whose countenance had the appearance of a Man ... "This is the Son of Man, who reveals all the treasures of that which is hidden because the Lord hath chosen Him ... and He will arouse the kings and the mighty ones from their couches, and the strong from their thrones ..." (xlviii. 3). "Before the sun and the constellations were created, before the stars of heaven were made, His name was named before the Lord of Spirits. He will be a staff to the righteous ... the light of the heathen, and the hope of those who are troubled in heart. All who dwell on earth will fall down and bow the knee before Him, and bless and laud and celebrate with song the Lord of Spirits. And for this reason hath He been chosen and hidden before Him from before the creation of the world, and for evermore." In Enoch, too, this Son of Man becomes Avenger and Hope of those whom the world persecutes, and it is God's wisdom who reveals Him and itself in Him. I have quoted this passage in order to show once and for all the link between John and the most sublime of contemporary thought, and also how far different from this is the Catholic dogma of the Second Person of the Holy Trinity made flesh for us that John proclaims.

At the head of the Apocalypse stands Christ, true God and true Man, to give it sanction. He utters that word which is "sharper than any two-edged sword, and pierces

---

continually associated, in the Apocalypse, the Person of the risen and triumphant Christ, the Lamb slain yet alive for evermore, with that of the Father, v. 9-13, etc. Thus does worship reveal as well as foster faith.

through even to the sundering of soul and spirit, of joints and marrow, and divides the desires and the thoughts of the heart" (Heb. iv. 12). The Apocalypse is that word, and who indeed would risk to blunt that sword?

II

THE LETTERS TO THE SEVEN CHURCHES
OF ASIA

THUS sanctioned, John composes the "covering letter" to the Church in Asia—for I have explained that the "Seven Churches" stands for the totality of Christians in the province—and in it he dwells, in the main, as he had been bidden, on "things present", their spiritual state and immediate prospects.

One preliminary word: What is the "angel" of the Church to whom John is bidden to write? Some modern critics have said the word should keep its literal meaning— "messenger". John was to write letters which messengers from these cities should take home. Frigid supposition; and how should such delegates be symbolized as stars in Christ's hand, while the Church itself is no more than a lampstand? The Greek Fathers, on the whole, saw in them the angel guardians of the Churches, like the "princes" in Daniel x. 13, etc. The Latin Fathers preferred to see in them the bishops of those Churches. All these explanations have their difficulty. The letters would seem to be to men, for they carry rebuke or encouragement. And the stars, which the angels are, shine pure and indefectible, though they are not the sun; while it is the lamp which may flicker and go out. Yet only in one doubtful passage of St. Paul, which gains colour from this very one of St. John, are bishops in the New Testament designated as angels. Nor should we altogether fear to hear angels rebuked and devoid of human characteristics, since Daniel himself seems to view the spiritual "princes" of Persia and Greece actually in conflict.

We hold, then, that St. John is not merely thinking of, or picturing, the several Churches—else he should have put, simply, "To the Church that is in Ephesus", etc., "write"—nor yet simply their bishops; nor yet simply an angel guardian. Is he not holding in his mind at least two "levels"—the human Church, existing in the concrete upon earth, and no doubt its bishop, though not so much officially as personifying, so to say, the special character and tendencies of his Church; *and* the heavenly prototype, the spiritual equivalent, the true spirit—the idea, Plato would have said—of the Church on earth? Rather so, in some Rabbinic writings, the true ark, the true furniture of the tabernacle, were conceived as existing in heaven, and to be but dimly imaged in the concrete objects of earthly worship. Dare we even think that he perceives almost the presence of Christ Himself, waxing and waning in the presence of His frail human representative, and of that community of Christians for whom that representative in his turn stood as symbol? Were this so, we should see John's gaze passing through every stage of reality from end to end—from the multiplicity of the faithful, through their representative bishop, through the spiritual world of ideals, to Christ Himself, at once Source of all life and pervasive life—above them wholly, in them partly, and longing to be in them yet more completely. Enough, perhaps, to see with Père Allo a "cascade" of symbolism moving from the star to the ideal Church, held firmly in Christ's hand, through the earthly summing-up of the Church— the bishop—to the concrete Church itself, the faithful, with all their faults. The realities are—Christ, the ideal Church, the concrete Church; the symbols—the sun, the star, the lamp.

The history of the city of Ephesus is fascinating and

very long. We cannot possibly relate it here. Enough to say that in St. John's time Ephesus was by far the most important of the Asiatic cities, not only in Christian history, but as governmental centre, as gate from Rome to the East and from the East to Rome, and commercially. The trade in "marble, vermilion, oils, and essences", gold and silver work, and the slave trade, kept it in touch with Italy, Greece, Egypt, Spain, and the Orient, and it was extremely rich. Its philosophical interests were of almost unshared antiquity, and in John's time it was thronged with schoolmasters and students. Above all, its worship of the prehistoric Asiatic nature-goddess, now invoked as Artemis—"the goddess whom all Asia and the civilized world worship" (Acts xix. 27)—and its enormous temple dominated popular imagination. To this worship had been quite early associated Cæsar-worship. A shrine and an altar of Augustus were placed in the temple of Artemis herself, and a coin finally shows no less than three official emperor-temples in close association with that of the national goddess.

In this overwhelming environment Christianity had maintained itself and merited John's praise: even, the Church there had been skilled to discern and reject those itinerant and unsanctioned "apostles" and "prophets" against whom warnings and even ecclesiastical legislation had soon enough to be directed. For, in the fluid state of much early Christian experience, it was easy for all sorts of charlatans or half-deluded enthusiasts to ape the divine mission. Yet the Ephesian Church had departed from the admirable fervour of Pauline days (Acts xix. 20; cf. Eph. i. 3). John warns them to repent and return, lest their lampstand be shifted from its place. But John has this to console him: "... that they hate the works of the Nicolaitans whom I also hate".

This sect or tendency reappears in the messages to Pergamum and Thyatira: its leaders taught men sensual sin and participation in food offered to idols. Like a new Balaam or a new Jezebel, the Nicolaitan reintroduced pagan practices and immoralities into God's Israel. Clearly no heretic even could openly teach immorality and idolatry and hope to get a hearing. What this school advised was a kind of "neutral" participation in the civic side of pagan worship—the great social banquets, for example, which followed the religious ceremonies and used the sacrificial foods. Yet not alone did these great feasts lead often enough to drunkenness and laxity, but— though it had long been recognized that to the Christian all foods are "clean"—so to participate in the feast created an impression at least that the participators were joining in the worship. John bade the Christian abstain altogether—a sterner command than at first sight we might think. Not only was he cutting off the Christian from those religious celebrations that made the very life of the place, but from all those guild and club feasts which were essential to its commercial life; for, without belonging to a trade-guild or club, success in business was impossible, and for a member abstention from these social celebrations was no less impossible; indeed, should he do well in his trade, he would be forced to take a lead in them. But into all alike some religious ceremonial entered, especially the worship of the Emperor. Needless to say the "broad-minded" would—how strongly and how plausibly!— have claimed a compromise. How exasperating and out of date the old regulation must have seemed; how desirable was tolerance even for the sake of the well-being and the spread of the influence of the Church!

But the Apostle is relentless. Let them hold firm; the conqueror shall have better foods than these—he shall eat of the Tree of Life that is in the Garden of God.

Are we to think that John, when threatening the shifting of the lampstand of the Ephesian Church, had in mind the fact that no city had been so forced—by reason of the continual silting up of its harbour, and for other causes—to change its site? Or that, when promising the fruit of the Tree of Life, he recalled that Ephesian coins bore the symbol of the sacred tree associated with the worship of the nature-goddess? This may seem far-fetched, though so rich are these letters in allusions to details drawn from the environment of the several Churches that the surmise is far from fantastic (ii. 1-7).

Next, John writes to Smyrna. This was a superb city, second only to Ephesus, cultured, religious, intoxicated with its own loveliness as coins prove; it was the "beauty-spot", the "idol" of Asia. Its games, too, were famous, though not to their conqueror's wreath should reference be found in the promise made to the Christian conqueror. That alludes rather to the "wreath" or "crown" of Smyrna —as the ring of buildings was known that flashed from the hills to the east—a metaphor so popular that much later on a speaker could pray for Smyrna a "wreath", not of palaces and porticoes merely, but of virtuous citizens. And so devoted an alliance bound the city to Rome that she had earned the proud surname of "the Faithful". St. John does not forget this when he closes his letter.

Smyrna's Church had already suffered and knew real poverty ("But thou art rich!" cries John), not because the majority of the faithful there were slaves, or unmoneyed, but because they were true to the laws that excluded them from so much that success implied, and also, it is clear, because of downright persecution from those Jews who were to egg on the populace to demand the death of St.

Polycarp. He may have been Bishop of Smyrna even at this date, for he died very old, being executed for refusing to say "Cæsar is LORD" during the games in honour of the Augusti in 155. "Jews?" John cries indignantly. "They are no Jews. A synagogue? Yes! A synagogue of Satan" (9). Worse was in store; but the persecution should be brief. Let them be faithful unto death, and they should receive the crown of life, and the body's death would but ensure that no second death should slay them. "Who", cried St. Paul, "shall separate us from the love of Christ?" Not any persecution nor death itself. Through these we are "more than conquerors". What separates man from man on earth does but knit us closer to the love of Jesus (8-11).

Pergamum was in a special way a focus of pagan worship. It was full of temples, and twice had won a title for its devotion to the emperor cult. Also it was the centre of the Asiatic cult of Asklepios, whose symbol, like that of "heroes" generally, was the serpent. But Asklepios was a beneficent hero, and his worship innocent; the conclusion of this letter, however, gains double significance when we learn that in the second century, at Pergamum, Aelius Aristides, after sleeping (according to the ritual) in Asklepios's shrine, received the "new name" of Theodoros— God's gift—together with a symbolic token which he carried about with him, drawing comfort from its sight when in trouble. But when John cries out, "I know where thou dwellest—where Satan's throne is"—he will scarcely so much have alluded to the ubiquitous serpent of the hero, as to the general religious importance of the city—it was the first to have erected a provincial temple to the Emperor—and especially to its enormous open-air altar of Olympian Zeus, visible from afar and dominating the whole plain.

Here too the Church had maintained its faith, and even

had had its martyr—Anteipas—whose name alone survives pathetically thus upon John's page. Yet in her, too, there was a modern Balaam, the sect of the Nicolaitans, or the actual leader of that lax way of thinking and acting, who taught the faithful to share the idol-feasts that led to lust (Num. xxxi. 16).

No! not that should be the conqueror's reward, but the manna "laid up" before God in the ark (Exod. xvi. 23: cf. Heb. ix. 4), which, Jewish tradition told, had been hidden till it should be restored to the people when Messiah should come—that bread from heaven of which John, too, should speak (Gospel, vi.); Jesus had promised it, and had said it was Himself; the eucharistic feast that the catacombs should portray in the likeness of the manna-jar; the this-life symbol of the supernatural union of man, through the Word-made-flesh, with God.

That union is again symbolized by the "white stone", or token, engraved with the new name that none could read save him who should receive it and Him who gave it. In widely diffused belief each person or even thing had its true secret self, to which belonged its true and secret name; who knew the name had power over the self. Here Christ gives it, and therefore knows it; and the victorious Christian knows it, and the two are united in one reciprocal life, to which all human life, how prosperous soever and successful, is "poor" and but half-illusory. But it is through St. John's Gospel that Our Lord most fully teaches this mystery of the new life (Apoc. ii. 12-17).

Thyatira, though a smaller town, and not known to have had an emperor temple, yet was commercially very active. It had guilds of bakers, dyers, tanners, clothiers, potters, wool-workers, linen-workers, shoe-makers, workers in bronze and others; and though these probably existed everywhere, yet here was enough, without any further

cause for anxiety, to distress the Christians. It was practically impossible, as I said, to exist in trade without belonging to a guild and sharing its social functions, annivers-
aries, and feasts. To such a fusion a self-styled prophetess,
a new Jezebel, incited the faithful—for it really looks as
though St. John meant more than that the laxists behaved
like the pagan queen of Israel, and is referring to a definite
woman. There was in Thyatira a shrine where an eastern
Sibyl lived and gave oracles; it is certain that the town
contained, later on, Montanist prophetesses; perhaps a
Nicolaitan prophetess tried to rival the Sibyl and antici-
pated the heretic mediums. Anyhow, the Thyatiran
Church seemed downright "wedded" to her teaching; its
angel is bidden to divorce her—she has had full opportunity to repent; this spiritual adulteress shall be placed
upon a bed—but of torment; and her children shall be
slain. The Church should know that Christ's keen eye
searches out the deepest roots and fibres of deceit; no
plausible mask, no sophistry, that He cannot penetrate.
"Deep things" she professed to teach to her inner circle of
initiates; a secret doctrine; a forerunner of the gnostic
theosophy, suited to the favoured few—"deep things, so
called and truly, but of Satan"; Satan's depths, not God's.
Later, this phrase—the depth, or deep things—became
popular among the gnostics, and in history this proud
claim to inner and subtler knowledge has always seemed to
ally itself to anarchy of life. The stern seer promises the
brow-beaten Thyatirans that they in their turn shall wield
Christ's iron-tipped shepherd's club; while, in place of
their lampstand's flickering wick, He shall give them that
Morning Star before which even the starry "angels" pale,
for it is Himself. Not until He come at the consummation
of all things is He the Sun in His strength. "Of old," says
St. Peter (2 Pet. i. 19), "you had the Word of Prophecy, to

which you did well to attend, as to a lamp shining in a dark place, till such time as the day break, and the Morning Star rise in your hearts." Him, then, the Thyatirans may forthwith possess; and "He who hath the Son hath life" (1 John v. 12); (18-29).

Sardis was a city whose glories belonged to ancient Lydian, and then to Persian, history, rather than to modern, though Tiberius had restored it after its ruin by earthquake in A.D. 17. Built on a hill that looked sheer and impregnable, but was made only of hardened mud, not rock, and crumbled under suns and rains, and left fissures whereby a Cyrus and an Antiochus were able to escalade and surprise it, like thieves in the night, it was particularly devoted to the Emperor. Yet its special cult was that of the ancient goddess of nature, here known as Cybele, and worshipped with peculiarly barbaric and hideous ritual. If it was to this moist and tainted atmosphere, sodden with sanctified licentiousness, that the local Christians had succumbed, small wonder that the Apostle rebukes them with terrible severity and, indeed, irony. Hitherto the phrase "I know thy works" had led to praise and congratulation. Here he exclaims:

> I know thy works, that thou hast the name of living—and thou art dead.

Yet perhaps the death was but sleep ... Let them awake, and establish what was left of their true life: empty were their works; few were the faithful.

> If thou wakest not, I will come like a thief, and in no wise shalt thou know the hour when I shall come at thee.

But to the conqueror He would give the white raiment of festivity and triumph, unbefouled by the blood and filth of that paganism in which they were expiring, and then their

names never at all would He blot out from the Book of
Life, but before God and angels would acknowledge
them (iii. 1-6).

Earthquake-racked Philadelphia was but a small city—
her timid population lived mostly outside the dangerous
walls—and her Church, too, was small and weak; but
was faithful, and Christ, who holds those keys that unlock
the gates of time and eternity, and is Master of His royal
house on earth and in heaven, has already flung open a
door for her influence. Here Jews again are the enemy; but
Christ promises that they shall come as suppliants to her,
and shall "know that I have loved thee". Persecution was
to come upon the whole known world, but she would be
safeguarded; and her conquerors were to be made pillars
in the Temple of God, the true new Temple, and thence
should never more be stirred; and on each pillar should be
engraved the name of God, the name of God's own city,
the New Jerusalem, and, He solemnly affirms, "My own
new name".

What is this mystery? John surely does not forget that
the city itself had received from the adopted son of
Tiberius, Germanicus, the "new name" of Neo-Cæsarea—
the New Cæsar-City; better than this should the new name
be that He would give to them. But more than that. The
pillar had played its important part in Jewish religious life;
even on the columns and tiles of pagan temples the name
of the divinity to whom they were dedicated was often
inscribed. The Philadelphians are God's unshakable
temple, sealed and signed as His. But even this falls short
of that vision in John's mind that was also in Paul's—of
that Temple coextensive with the whole new Holy City, the
Church Catholic, wherein not alone does the Word-made-
flesh impart a new way of *being* to those who are now
incorporate with Him, but even for Himself He acquires a

new title—dare we say a new self, since, without them, He would not be what He is? The pillars are not the temple, yet without them the temple cannot stand. Without the head the body dies, yet without the limbs the head is meaningless. Without us for Sons of God, He had not been the Firstborn among many brethren; without the saved, not Jesus (7-13).

Laodicea was a proud and self-sufficient city. Already in the year 60, after a fierce earthquake, she had refused help from Rome, and had rebuilt herself, as Tacitus relates, "from her own resources, without any help from us". The town was full of gold, banks, and money-exchanges. One of its industries was a black and glossy wool; another, the fabrication of the "Phrygian powder", collyrium, which was applied to sore eyes and exported throughout the Roman world; and, full in view of the town, the hot springs of Hierapolis tumbled down their cliff, to flow, tepid and nausea-provoking, through the Lycus valley.

To the Church of Laodicea John sends a terrible message, in the Name of Christ, whose total and all-pervasive personality he solemnly sets at the head of what he writes:

Thus speaketh
The Amen,
The Witness faithful and true,
The Origin of the creation of God.
I know thy works,
That thou art neither hot nor cold;
Would that thou wert cold or hot!
But now that thou art tepid, and neither hot nor cold,
I am about to vomit thee out of My mouth.
Thou sayest:
"I am wealthy! I have made my money!
I have need of nothing!"
And knowest not

That *thou* art the wretched, and pitiable, and a pauper, and
   blind, and naked.
I counsel thee
That thou buy from ME
Gold purified by fire that thou mayest grow wealthy,
And white raiment that thou mayest gird thyself,
That the shame of thy nakedness be not seen,
And eyesalve, to put it on thine eyes, that thou mayest see.

But the terrible Apocalyptist was, too, the Apostle of
Christ's love. He resumes:

Whom I love, them I rebuke and chasten.
Be fervent, then, and repent.
See—I am standing at the door and am knocking ...
If any man hear My voice, and open the door,
Then will I come in to him,
And eat with him,
And he with Me.
The conqueror—to him will I give to sit upon My throne,
Even as I did conquer and did take My seat
With My Father, upon His throne.
He who can hear, let him hear
What the Spirit is saying to the Churches (14-22).

Very briefly, what are the main impressions disengaged
from these letters? First, the life of these Christian communities in their environment—simple folk for the most
part; slaves in high percentage; trading folk at any rate,
finding it necessary to apply ruthlessly to their daily life
principles that had no sanction save spiritual ones, and
brought no material compensations at all. Doubtless,
within each family Christian belief forged links of love in-
comparably more sweet because more pure, and at all
times blessed by the felt presence of the Lord; doubtless
too, each Christian household found, in the help gladly
given by its neighbour, and in the sacred and half-secret

association of their common worship, that where but two or three of the faithful were gathered together, there was Christ in the midst of them. But such human happiness as this included was on the whole the echo, the reflection, of these spiritual consolations, which assuredly needed to be more frequent and preternatural among men on whom all that was natural bore so hardly. Poor, few relatively, having to exclude themselves from so much social merriment and ordinary intercourse, regarded consequently as morose and aloof, deliberate pariahs and aliens; dangerous even; grudging and ready to destroy what they would not join in; anarchists and atheists, they were elsewhere called; bewildered and intimately hurt, again, by those of their own number who—small wonder—felt that such a life was surely grown intolerable, and who on fair excuses made their compromise with paganism, and prospered, yet precisely at the cost of what alone, the faithful felt, and as St. John averred, could keep inspiration high and conscience pure.

And if, in the great towns, worship of gods grown Romanized or Hellenized, though really native and originally half savage, seemed impressive rather by its social and political importance, its gorgeous ritual, its ubiquity, its wealth; and if here or there the vast crowded temples of an Artemis, a Zeus, an Asklepios, seemed established, surely, for ever and ever, yet in the remoter mountain towns the primitive barbarity of cult had, too, its mystic spell for men whose temperament, after all, had not been abolished by conversion—the sheer fascination of the ancient, of the horrible, and the very defiance of that nature that it worshipped and mutilated; the frenzied, yet drugging influence of cymbal and of horn; the infectious rhythm of wanton swaying dance; the intoxication of sheer blood, as the fanatics of Cybele advanced, grotesquely

painted, scourging their red shoulders. And over everything, in city, town, and field, brooded the incarnate
majesty of Rome, the divine invisible Emperor, who
gathered into his hands every thread and towards whom
all life inevitably set. The serene gods of Greece, the
strange, hypnotic imageries of the Asiatic cults, the tremendous, unconquerable Emperor—these ruled the religious atmosphere in which the Christian faith sought to
survive, gasping at times for breath, fainting and reviving.

The second great impression is that of John's own
personality. You might imagine that in ecstasy personality
would vanish. Not so. See Catherine; see Teresa. And
here, together with the tremendous effect produced of
authority, of unflinching government, of austere rejection
of the plausible compromise, of sheer fierce hate, less for
the honest paganism that no Christian could mistake than
for the insinuating poisonous influence of a Christian sick
to death and tainting the Christian life at large, and for the
Jew, apostate from his own history of divine predilection
and mission—nay, the inflexible adversary from the
beginning of his own Messiah; together, then, with this
calm knowledge of his right to rule the province, goes a
tenderness that surely thrills us. Never is John merely hard
or fanatical, never querulous or piqued. He knows what
the Churches are going through.

> I know thy works; I know thine affliction and thy poverty;
> but thou art rich. I know where thou dwellest—where
> Satan's throne is.

All the minutest details of their condition he has observed,
and in exile he remembers and alludes to them, and applies
them in most delicate manner to their present state. True,
it is of their spiritual life that, of course, he thinks most
eagerly of all. Those promises with which each message

closes are not conventional or haphazard symbolism, the ready-made assurance of ultimate reward hung out by a preacher to an audience who has nothing to hope from the present. They tremble with passionate conviction, they reveal the focus of all his truest life. So sure is he of it that he has no hesitation in transferring thither the whole of his Christians' consolation; his own supreme happiness will be to triumph in the full presence of Christ among these His children, who are his own. The heart of John, like the heart of Paul, is great and glorious, and tender and yearning and human and full of God; and these two men, so different in almost every other way, should ever be kept side by side, and studied in that which utterly unites them, the triumphant love of Christ in their human hearts.[1]

The last impression that remains ineffaceable is that of the eternal Son of God, Christ living in His Church, moving about among the seven lamps. We may own at once that the figure of the great initial vision is not that, simply, of the human Jesus, the little child of Mary, the working man of Nazareth; Jesus tired and hungry, heartbroken, or exultant in His living and His dying; not even the Jesus of the forty days of risen but still earthly life. Yet from the vision of this Alpha and Omega, Source of all creation and its Amen; Him whose word is a fiery sword, whose hand holds masterfully all spirits, whose eyes strike even saints, half-fainting, to the earth; eternal Power, eternal Wisdom,

[1] Had St John read St Paul's epistles? Surely. But it would take long to indicate the many tiny touches which suggest what in itself cannot but be true. I will but allude to iii. 14, where John uses almost word for word Paul's expression in Col. i. 15. John is writing to the Laodiceans, and Paul to the Colossians hard by, and his letter was meant to be read by the Laodiceans too. It would be harder to show that John uses the Synoptic Gospels, though it could be argued. Yet I cannot but recall that "I will not cast upon you any other burden", in ii. 24, where he is warning the Thyatirans to avoid pagan feasts, is just what was said at Jerusalem on the same subject (Acts xv. 28), and after all John was present at that council and shared in the drawing up of that decree.

thrilling Omnipresence—not from all this are eliminated the humanity and death, the tenderness, pathos, and the Friend. Intimacy is the best proof of love, union, and communion. Not once alone are love and its great work— redemption at the price of life-blood—made mention of; but beyond this, what is not implied, with awestruck reticence and the half-silences of ecstasy, what is not revealed by those promises wherein Christ gives Himself to Christian, and knits Christian into Christ! He gives that Morning Star which is Himself, and it shines within each heart. Into that Temple which is Himself He builds the chosen columns; He creates for each alike the new name, and on His side receives His own new name. Near Him they will be, with a nearness too near for imagination to master, when they sit on His throne, which is God's; and should the sublimity of that dazzlement terrify the shrinking soul into St. Peter's "Depart from me: I am a sinful man", there is that other intimacy—Christ comes; He stands at the door; He knocks. He enters, and in the secret communion of two, Friend and friend, that feast is *offered to Him* in which *He* is the food, and life springs for both from the one source. *Quis separabit? Vivo iam non ego.*

The sternest of all rebukes ends in the offer of the incomparable love feast.

III

THE APOCALYPSE OF THE FUTURE

The Twofold Prefatorial Vision

I. (i).

To the revelation of "things present" is now to be added that of "what must be hereafter". John will contemplate the whole universe, but it is from heaven that he will see it; and to the visions of the divine-human history of earth is prefixed the spectacle of the calm majesty of the eternal. A door in heaven is opened, and John is bidden "Come up hither", and is forthwith "in the Spirit" or in ecstasy.

(*a*) Behold, a throne in heaven; and on the throne One seated. He who sat was like the crystal and the ruby to behold; and in a circle round the throne a rainbow like emerald to see. And round about the throne thrones four-and-twenty; and upon the thrones four-and-twenty aged men clothed in white garments, and upon their heads golden crowns.

And from out of the throne come lightnings and voices and thunders.

And seven lamps burning before the throne, which are the seven spirits of God.

And before the throne, as it were, a sea of glass like crystal; and in front of the throne and around it four living beings, full of eyes before and behind. The first was like to a lion; the second to a young bull; the third had his countenance like a man's; the fourth was like an eagle in his flight. Each of them had six wings; they were full of eyes, round about and within, and make no pause, day nor night, saying:

Holy, Holy, Holy Lord, God, All-Governor, who wast,

who art, who art to come. And when those beings give glory
and honour and thanksgiving to Him who is seated upon the
throne, who liveth for the ages of the ages, then do the four-
and-twenty aged men fall down before Him who is seated on
the throne, and do adore Him who liveth to the ages of the
ages, saying:

Worthy art Thou, O Lord and God of us, to accept the
glory and the honour and the power, for Thou didst create
all things, and owing to Thy will they had being and were
created (iv. 1-11).

In this picture of the eternal worship of heaven John
uses ancient and consecrated symbolism. Ezekiel, too, had
seen the heavenly throne, ringed with rainbow, and Him
who was there seated; only John refrains from those
human features under which Ezekiel pictures Him, and
here, as not seldom hereafter, will refrain even from nam-
ing Him. And that "sea" of pure crystal flooding round the
Dweller in "light inaccessible" is, in Daniel's vision (vii.
10), a fiery stream; in Ezekiel God is throned above a
"firmament" like, first, to "the terrible crystal", but again
to the sapphire stone (i. 22, 26), that "work of the bright
sapphire, as it were the very heaven for clearness", upon
which the feet of Yahweh rested over Sinai (Exod. xxiv.
10). For, to the Hebrew imagination, the sky arched in a
solid vault above the earth, and in the waters it upheld
above it were planted the foundations of the throne of God
(Gen. i. 6, 7; Job xxxvii. 18, etc.).

Before the throne, and *within* that "sea" outside whose
insuperable flood all the rest has its being, are the Seven
Spirits of God, not therefore assuredly seven angels, however high in dignity or expressive of the spiritual world as a
whole, but the third Person of the Most Holy Trinity
Himself, seen, as before, in His sevenfold or universal
operation.

It is then, I think, that we must see the heavenly senate—
the four-and-twenty aged men, seated in a ring around the
Centre of all things. What, then, are they? It has become
customary to see in them the twelve Patriarchs and twelve
Apostles, and in a sense this is surely so. But scarcely just
as the historical twenty-four. Else John, who was one of
them, would be seen doing himself homage. Besides, in
this vision is nothing that is earthly as such. May they not,
then, be like the stars or the angels of the Churches, the
celestial prototypes of that enduring Church that God has
chosen and that has triumphed? We cannot but connect
the number twenty-four at least to some extent with John's
other uses of the number twelve where this relates to the
Apostles, and also recall his conviction of the continuity of
the true Synagogue and Church. But I see no reason why
the twenty-four should not be at once angels in the sense of
the first vision, and the Patriarchs and Apostles, as existing
in the eternal plan of God, and ultimately the whole body
of the elect.

An outermost circle is formed by the four beings, of all
that St. John has said so far the hardest to visualize. They,
too, are ancient symbols, though as usual John simplifies
and thereby beautifies them. In Ezekiel, too, are flashing
lamps or torches moving swiftly to and fro among the four
beings, to *each* of which the prophet attributes the four
faces, lion's, eagle's, bull's, and human. Ezekiel, indeed,
was idealizing what he had seen in his Babylonian exile;
his mysterious four-winged creatures are like those animal
supports that upheld the platform on which a king's
throne rests, and they, too, move hither and thither on
wheels, though a spirit is in them and the wheels themselves
are full of eyes. Perhaps Ezekiel attached no very definite
detailed meaning to his strange creations: they may have
been but spiritualized, "heavenlied" versions of what had

struck his eyes as so strange; nor perhaps ought we to press even John's details too closely. But for many reasons I think we may agree that these four represent God's immanent power and wisdom, active in all created nature —notice that this vision is precisely the undying worship paid by all *creation* to God—or, if you will, nature in its heavenly ideal offering its homage to its Maker and Preserver, its Source and End. The universe in this sense is ever wakeful, ever consciously wanting and worshipping its God.

Here, then, in one adoration of God the visible universe, the human race, and the world of pure spirits harmoniously unite; and it is Isaiah's hymn they chant:

"I saw Yahweh seated upon a throne, high and lifted up; and His train filled the temple"—that Temple which is now the world, and indeed ever was, and in all its parts the very skirts of the robe of God. "Above Him stood the seraphim; each one had six wings ... and one cried unto another, saying: Holy, Holy, Holy is the Lord of Hosts: the fulness of the whole earth is His glory" (vi. 1, 3). Nor, ever since, has the liturgy ceased from that hymn.

(*b*) After the revelation of heaven's undying worship, and of the eternal total harmony into which are gathered up earth's scattered prayers, John's eye reverts to the events of time, though still under the light, in the atmosphere, so to speak, of eternity, summing up history into a universal and all but simultaneous vision.

He sees a scroll, written on back and front, as was the way when the crowded contents overran the limits of the parchment. It is sealed up with seven seals; and not in heaven, nor earth, nor hell, has one been capable of breaking them, of unrolling the scroll and mastering its contents. The scroll contains the history of all that is—the total enigma; that which no created intelligence can ever understand. The world, indeed, has despaired when it has gazed merely on its own mystery.

But one of the elders of that Church to which is granted to bring God's revelation to mankind bids John not to weep; for the Prophesied and Promised, the Lion of Judah, the Messiah, David's Son, has conquered, and shall break the seals and read the book.

And lo! no Lion, but a Lamb—a Lamb before the throne, where the Seven Spirits are; a Lamb standing, though slain; a Sacrifice in whom, despite the imperishable wounds, is fulness of power and wisdom (for such is the right meaning of the seven horns and seven eyes), a creative power and wisdom, for these are the Seven Spirits, that is, the Holy Spirit, pervading and giving life and meaning to the earth.

He comes, and takes from the hand of the Creator the book that He has written; and music of harp and fragrance of incense rises in the celestial liturgy, and a New Song is sung by Nature and by Church:

> Worthy art Thou to take the book and to open its seals, because Thou wast slain and didst buy men to God at the price of Thy blood from every tribe and tongue and people and nation, and didst make them a kingdom unto God, and priests, and they shall be kings upon the earth.

And a great shout of angels round the throne—"ten thousand times ten thousand, thousands of thousands"—echoes them:

> Worthy is the Lamb that is slain to receive the power and riches and wisdom and strength and honour and glory and praise.

And with men and angels, "every created thing that is in the heaven, or upon the earth, and underneath the earth, yea, all that is in them'', all creation, then, to its outer-most rings, joins in the great ascription:

> To Him that is seated upon the throne, and to the Lamb, the praise and the honour and the glory and the might, to the ages of the ages.

And the four speak their amen, and the four-and-twenty prostrate themselves and worshipped (v. 1-14).

When David placed the Ark in the tabernacle, he bade the people sing:

> Save us, O God of our Salvation,
> And gather us together and deliver us from the heathen,
> To give thanks unto Thy holy name,
> And to triumph in Thy praise.
> Blessed be Yahweh, the God of Israel,
> From everlasting even to everlasting.
>
> (1 Par. xvi. 35.)

Such was the conclusion of the song by which David celebrated Yahweh on the day when His dwelling-place was finished. Such the ancient hymn of praise; and how far poorer, for all its splendid exultation, than the apocalyptic pæan, offered before that throne which God and the true Son of David share, They who, as the Seer will tell us, *are* heaven's temple, a temple inclusive, indeed, of all that is, since naught that is escapes Their infinite presence.

So in these two visions we have heard a double praise—the eternal *sanctus* whereby the eternal God is hymned by His creation as, in His all-wisdom, He planned it, and as, in its consummation, it shall be; and the new *gloria* by which redeemed humanity, nay, the angelic host itself, extols that Victim who, in time, was slain, and, in eternity, is living; the Son of God, made flesh, dying, and arisen, who alone can solve the riddle of all history, since its solution is none other than Himself—nay, without Him that history could not even have been written. So God has willed. Without the Incarnation, the world, its process, and its destiny, have, in the full supernatural sense, no value nor significance.

These two visions, then, are, as it were, the summing-up of all existence—the Uncreated, and the created in its ultimate relation to the eternal. We pass now to visions of the operation of, as it were, enduring laws or tendencies in the general history of the Creation.

Part A I. (ii): The Seven Seals
One by one, then, the seals are to be broken.
(a) The First Four Seals (vi. 1-9)

The first seal is broken. One of the four cries, "Come!" And a white horse moves across the field of John's vision. His rider holds a bow, and the conqueror's wreath is given to him, and he rides on, "conquering and to conquer".

The second seal: the summons again; a blood-red horse; and his rider has leave to rob the earth of peace, and to make men slay one another; and in his hand a great sword.

The third seal: "Come." And a black horse. His rider holds a balance; and a voice explains this symbol, else too obscure. For a day's wage a day's food shall be obtainable —one measure of wheat, or three of the coarser barley-grain; the olive-oil and the vintage shall go unharmed.

But the fourth seal summons a horse that is pale, or wan; Death rides him; and power is given them over the quarter of the earth, to slay by famine and pestilence and savage beasts.

The prophet Zechariah had seen in vision four horses (i. 8, 10, and vi. 1-8), with horses red, white, black, and grizzled. They were the four winds of the Lord, who went forth to execute God's judgment on the earth.[1] And in Ezek. xiv. 21 God will send His four dreadful judgments upon Jerusalem—sword, famine, pestilence, and wild beasts.

Let us, then, begin with what is clear. An outraged Nature summons God's judgment upon the earth—for the word ἔρχου, "Come", signifies in the Apocalypse, always, the coming of God or Christ: had the summons been addressed to the seer or to the horseman the word used would have been δεῦρο.[2] And in various guises it appears. The blood-red horse is easy to understand. This is the curse of war, from which the Empire scarcely for an hour was free. And the pale horse is clear.[3] Death and the world of the dead are his rider and his train; death by the sword and by famine and by pestilence. The social order crashes, and with it civilization; beasts return to the haunts of men. And yet, John reminds us, the world still goes on—only a fraction of it is destroyed. And the black horse? Is the dearth he symbolizes downright famine? But famine with its attendant plague are the share of the pale horseman. Surely we are told that the prevalent social state is such that men do not indeed *starve*—all the necessities of life are there to be had; but for bare sustenance men have to pay their all—a day's wage for the strict minimum of

[1] The winds played a great role in apocalyptic; they were half-personified, and numbers of instances from the Old Testament itself could be quoted of the service that God exacts from them.

[2] Notice that in a sense the original picture is not carried through. Until *all* the seals are broken, the scroll cannot be read. But this were to misuse our material. As each seal is broken, John conceives himself as seeing part of the world's contents and their significance.

[3] The Greek says, "a green horse". The symbolism is intolerable, or grotesque, to us. But what is meant is the colour of corruption.

food. Astonishing comment on the manner of life—inhuman, and thus unjust—which the masses of the Empire led.

What, then, of the white horse? I hold that it means that Empire—which, to a contemporary, seemed nearly all the world that counted—in which these things happen; or, shall I say, that *imperialism* which made them bound to happen? John sees the empire of the earth, *the would-be self-sufficient cosmos*, shining in victorious white, crowned and armed, conquering and destined yet to conquer; but a cosmos which, in so far as godless, breeds chaos; involves bloodshed continually, and even for those who are not actually at war, a sordid life of toil, and grey impotence even to rise above the mere living it, a peace as bad as war; a social order bound to crash down into the accumulated woes that John finally portrays.[1]

Thus closes the series of the first four seals. But there is more in the world than worldliness. There is in it, too, a continual tendency to *surmount* the world—a tendency which leads through tragedy temporal to eternal triumph; the everlasting Victim reproduces Himself and His history in His associates.

---

[1] It has been argued that the white horse means militarism. But war belongs to the red horse. And the *triumphator* did not ride on a white horse, but in a four-horse chariot. Still, white is the colour of victory. I hardly think that because in apocalyptic imagery it is nearly always used in a favourable meaning, it need always be so. The picture in John's eye is far rather of those mounted gods which were so common in Asia: the Empire was just such a false god. It has also been held that the rider on the white horse is the Word of God Himself (see xix. 11 sqq.). But I cannot bring myself to think that John would have put Our Lord Himself so absolutely on a level with three abstractions, nor assimilated His coming so completely to three comings that were nothing but disaster. No. The world's empire is the would-be substitute for, and in fact the parody of, the eternal kingdom and its King. I submit that John sees the heavenly counterpart of nature summon into the world the God whom nature, as it was, so utterly rejected, and then sees in four great visions the conditions of that world which were so many challenges rather than invitations to the coming of Christ.

(b) *The Fifth and Sixth Seals* (9-17)

The breaking of the fifth seal displays the altar.[1] Beneath it are the souls of those slain for the word of God and the witness they had given, that is, by their rejection of Cæsar-worship and refusal to apostatize, and for their loyalty to the Gospel and to the name of Jesus.[2] They cry insistently to God to vindicate their blood; and to each is given the "white robe" significant of his personal victory, and they are bidden "rest" yet for a little while, till those who, like them, are destined to be martyred should fulfil their course and make the reckoning complete. Then shall be the public recognition and God's great approval.

Here, then, are the martyrs under Nero, bidden to rest in peace till that not distant hour when the victims of Domitian shall be added to their number. But, more widely, John broods on the long tedium of the world's endurance, and the never complete, never categorical victory of right. "How long, Thou God holy and true?" is a cry that the faithful of all ages have reiterated; and built, it would seem, upon the foundations of the world is that altar of burnt-offering on whose base is spilled the life-blood of those who, wittingly or unwittingly, have served the Cross. Yet, refocussing our gaze on the immediate, we can see, buried already in the dark catacombs, the martyrs whose very tombs were used for altars, and over whose ashes was offered that undying Sacrifice with which their own was mingled, and that was powerful for their peace.

[1] Not *an* altar, but the altar that will be mentioned in ch. viii. John had not spoken of it when he related the worship of heaven in ch. iv., as though he had all his symbolic material in his eye all the while, but now forgets, as it were, that he had not actually mentioned this part of it. *He* has all his symbolic material at his disposal throughout, and feels as if his readers had the complete picture too.

[2] St. Polycarp (*Mart.*, 9) was bidden (i) to adore Cæsar, and (ii) to blaspheme Christ.

From the prayer of the martyrs and the promise of God, John causes our minds to pass at once to the fulfilment. The sixth seal is opened, and the death of the world's triumphant order is seen. When the world should die, Hebrew apocalypse had always foreseen the ruin of the solid firmament itself. Yahweh's coming should shake heaven and earth and sea (Agg. ii. 7); Joel, as St. Peter quoted (ii. 30-31; Acts ii. 19), had foretold Yahweh's wonders in the heavens and the earth—blood and fire and pillars of smoke. "The sun shall be turned into darkness and the moon into blood, before the great and terrible day of Yahweh come." Isaias (xxxiv. 4) had watched the mountains melt away, and all the starry host of heaven mouldering away, and the heavens rolled together like a scroll:

> And all their host shall fade away, as the leaf fadeth from the vine, and as a fading leaf from the fig-tree:

and of this traditional symbolism Our Lord Himself did not disdain to make use:

> "The sun shall be darkened and the moon shall not give her light, and the stars shall be fallen from the sky, and the powers in the sky shall be shaken." (Mark xiii. 24-5; Matt. xxiv. 29; Luke xxi. 25-6).[1]

So the sixth seal shows to John an earthquake, the sun sackcloth black, and the moon like blood, and the stars falling from the sky like unripe figs from storm-scourged

[1] So little are each of these details to be stressed, and a separate meaning attached to each, that not only can the Preacher say (Eccles. xii. 2) that, for the aged, sun and moon and stars "grow dark"; but the phrases passed into ordinary funeral inscriptions, and a Jewish epitaph of the Middle Ages describes the heavens in sackcloth, the stars in mourning, the hills shaken, all Israel in appalment, on the death day of him who was there buried. It was in these phrases that was traditionally, with full Hebrew hyperbole, described the end of a man, or of a nation, or of the world.

fig-trees; and the sky split asunder, and, like a torn scroll, rolled up this side and that; and mountains and islands ruined and in chaos. And kings and the chiefs of government and army and of commerce, yes, slave and free alike, shall cower into caves and call on the rock to hide them from the face of Him who is seated on the throne and from the wrath of the Lamb.

For the great and terrible day of His wrath is come, and who can stand firm?

So Nahum once had cried (i. 5-6):

The mountains quake before Him and the hills melt;
And the earth is upheaved at His presence,
Yea, the world and all who dwell therein.
Who can stand before His indignation?
And who can abide the fierceness of His anger?
His fury is poured out like fire,
And the rocks are broken asunder by Him.

And Malachi (iii. 2):

Who may abide the day of His coming?
And who shall stand when He appeareth?

St. Luke (xxi. 36) had heard men bidden to "watch and pray", that so indeed they might stand; and it is to those who "stood" that John's vision passes.

(c) A Double Vision Interposed (vii. 1-17)

The series of catastrophic visions is, as it were, now checked. The Sibylline Oracles (viii. 204) tell of a final storm that shall devastate the universe. John, on his side, sees four angels, masters of the four winds, holding them in, a pause before the hurricane destined to plunge upon the earth from all quarters of the world at once. An angel from the sunrise—the place of hope and renewal—was bidding them wait, for he held the signet of the living God, and not all His servants had been sealed upon their foreheads. The sealed should be exempted from, not the catastrophe, but from succumbing to the catastrophe. Such signing, or branding, was not uncommon in the Roman world: servants, soldiers, and criminals were thus marked upon their flesh, and in many ways this vision looks forward to episodes placed later in the book, as of the branding of the worshippers of the Wild Beast—Satan's Church —with his mark. And again it looks back to the exempting mark of the blood upon the doors of the exempted Israel when Egypt's first-born were to perish; and we cannot forget that very early indeed both Baptism and Confirmation were known as the sealing of the soul for God.[1]

John sees first the sealing of twelve times twelve thousand, chosen from the twelve tribes of Israel.[2] That number stands, it will be seen, for an indefinitely large yet perfect one; vast will be this multitude, yet none shall be left out. "Of those whom Thou hast given Me have I lost not one." Are they, then, those of the Chosen People who, after all, in whatever period of the world's history, had accepted Christ? It is certain that John loved his people, that he saw the Jewish Church and the Christian as in truth continuous, and that he knew well enough that the power of Christ reached backwards into the past as well as towards the

[1] It will be noticed that this system of dividing a group of seven into two groups of four and three respectively, and then of dividing the three into two and one by means of a double vision, is quite regular in the Apocalypse. The 4 : 3 plan could even be shown in the Letters to the Churches. But none the less such groups are closely interconnected, and the Apocalypse as a whole is no less firmly articulated and organic. This, to my mind, is by itself enough to prove its unity of authorship. But it would be impossible to display all these minutiæ in detail.

[2] Why does he leave out Dan? Impossible to be sure. He had to omit one name, since he distinguishes the tribe of Joseph from that of Manasses, and could not exceed the number twelve. There was a tradition that Antichrist should come from Dan, but that scarcely enters here.

future. The Lamb had been slain from the beginning of the world. Among the Jews there had been and must now be many thousands who looked, and look, forward to Him who is "the desire of the eternal hills", and even outside the Chosen People how many in all generations had darkly yearned for Him! Not irresponsive has He been to the inarticulate outcry of His creatures.

> Perchance after all they pursue, not what they deem, nor yet what they would say, but the Selfsame. For all things have by nature somewhat that is of God.

So wrote the pagan Aristotle, and grace is not narrower than his dream.

For my part, then, I think this vision is that of the Chosen People who have been faithful to their vocation— even so, a small number compared to the vast throngs of redeemed whom John now sees, elect from all the world.

For in the next part of this double vision expectant humanity is shown to itself as transfigured before its passion; or, if you will, the triumph is displayed by anticipation for their encouragement; or again, if you will, the real reality, hidden still yet actual—we *are* sons of God: heaven is but grace and its fruits made permanent and manifest.

And so lovely is this vision, so perfect are the words in which John clothes it—though in his strong ecstasy he here cares less, perhaps, than ever for the very laws of language[1]—that no comment of ours should risk its disfigurement.

> After this I saw—and look! a great multitude, that no man might number it, from every nation and tribes and

---

[1] I do not allude to his admirable paradoxes—the Blood that washes white, the Lamb that is a Shepherd—but to his broken syntax and heedlessness even of consecutive grammatical formations.

peoples and tongues—and they standing before the throne and before the Lamb. I saw them robed in white raiment, and palms are in their hands.

And all the angels had taken their stand in a ring around the throne and the four-and-twenty aged men and the four living beings, and they fell down before the throne upon their faces and adored God, saying:

Amen! The praise and the glory and the wisdom and the thanksgiving and the honour and the power and the strength to our God, unto the ages of the ages. Amen. And one of the aged men enquired of me:

These that are arrayed in white robes, who are they, and whence have they come? And I said to him: My lord, thou knowest. And he said to me: These are they who are coming from the great affliction; and they did wash their robes and make them white in the Blood of the Lamb. Therefore are they before the throne of God, and serve Him day and night in His temple, and He who is seated upon the throne shall spread His tent above them. They shall hunger no more, neither thirst any more, nor shall the sun strike upon them nor any scorching heat. For the Lamb that is before the throne shall shepherd them and shall lead them to fountains of living waters; and God shall wipe away every tear from their eyes.

(d) The Seventh Seal (viii. 1)

There follows one of the most solemn moments of the Apocalypse.

The seventh seal is opened; the book can be unrolled and read to the very end.

But there are no voices and no thunders; no calls, nor cries, nor visions.

"There was silence in heaven for about half an hour." Is there here, then, that incommunicable secret that "no man knoweth, neither the angels, nor the Son, but the Father only"? Is this that innermost heaven in which Paul heard spoken things ineffable? That for which all symbols have become vain, the perfect Word whereof all scattered talk is idle; that consummation of the All that neither eye hath seen nor ear heard, neither hath it entered into the heart of man to conceive? What no apocalypse can reveal?

Yes, that is no doubt true. Were the visions to close here that would be all the truth. But remember, what we have been reading of so far is the celestial version, shown under its suited symbols, of that which we are to re-see, though still under symbols, as accomplishing itself upon earth. In one sense we have seen everything; in another we have now to begin to see. Just as the visions do not present, within each a group, a mere time sequence, but show things that must be conceived as coexisting, so the great groups themselves are not visions of events that occur one after the other—as though when the seals were broken the seven trumpets are to be blown, and again later on the seven bowls outpoured; but these things happen upon different yet interpenetrating planes, and we are now to see, after the mysterious pause of the seventh seal, God's judgment working itself out in no skyey region, but upon earth.

PART A II: THE SOUNDING OF SEVEN TRUMPETS

(i) *The Double Prefatory Vision* (viii. 2-5)

(*a*) This strange vision reveals a new element in the equipment of the heavenly temple—an altar of incense, to which one of the seven angels that stand before God's face carries live coal from the altar of sacrifice. He places the coal upon the incense, and with the smoke the prayers of all the faithful ascend to God.

(*b*) Then what remains of the fire he casts upon the earth, and upon the earth the effects of the prayers are visible. The Godward strain bends back and alters human history. At last the silence is broken—first by thunders and cosmic uproar, then by the sounding of seven trumpets placed in the hands of the seven angels.

(ii) *The Seven Trumpets*

(*a*) *A Group of Four Trumpets* (6-13).—As each trumpet sounds some new chastising of the earth's wickedness is shown; yet the trumpets are not wholly signs of wrath, for precisely in those chastisements is involved the righteous judgment of God and the triumph of the saints.

A "third part"—that is, much, yet not all nor even most —of the earth's vegetation is destroyed by a hail mingled with fire and blood. Then of the sea a third part becomes blood; of fish and the crews of ships a third part perishes, for a blazing mountain is cast into it. A star, named *Absinthos*, or Wormwood, flaring like a lamp, falls into the "third part" of the fresh waters of the earth. Men die of these embittered waters. Finally, the third part of the sun and of the moon and of the stars is blighted, so that the day is bright only for the third part of itself and the night likewise.

Considering the book for the moment as sheer literature —and this scenic symbolism asks to be so regarded—we cannot deny that this part is less impressive than the preceding chapters. The four horses and their riders had a sinister and transcendent value, with a meaning not hard to decipher attached; while here all that we see is that nature in four of her departments—earth, sea, fresh waters, and sky—is sorely stricken. Since we cannot assign any separate meaning to the four events, we are forced to try to picture them, and that we can scarcely do. These "thirds" of sea and waters cannot be visualized.

Why did John write thus? It were jejune to seek for the origin of his symbols in natural facts that he had observed merely. He may certainly have witnessed an Ægean thunderstorm, in which the rain was reddened with fine sand from the Sahara; he may have heard of or even seen an eruption like that of Vesuvius in 79, or that which was to form a new island in 196. He may have watched, too, some notable meteor. But no celestial eclipse could account for the fourth portent.

St. Irenæus already saw clearly that John's mind has travelled back to the plagues of Egypt. John adds to the hail and fire of Exodus the blood which the Sibylline Oracles (v. 377) also mingle with the lightning. Enoch (xviii. 13) saw "seven stars like great mountains on fire", and Jeremiah (li. 25) compares hostile Babylon to a blazing mountain. If St. John already had the symbol of Babylon, which he is soon to use, in his mind, or even written down, this symbol may here have presented itself to him by association of ideas. It may, too, be noticed that here, as so often, he says that what he saw was *like* a mountain—*as if* a mountain—and indicates quite clearly how approximate only he feels his symbolism to be to its corresponding reality. Falling stars again were common enough as end-of-the-world symbols or portents; only the name Wormwood is strange as applied to this one. It has been pointed out that the perversion of justice (Amos v. 7, vi. 13), the fruits of idolatry (Deut. xxix. 18), divine chastisements generally (Jer. ix. 15), are in the Hebrew Bible described as "wormwood". But in reality, not because the star is Wormwood are the waters embittered, but because the waters were made bitter and deadly does John give to the star the name of that which would make them so. The corruption, not its cause, is the point of his attention. We cannot press the fact that the third part of the waters actually *become* wormwood, else it were impressive to perceive that while God can lift nature into the realm of supernature, yet the misuse of nature by sin can make its innocent elements into a source of poison and of death.

An eagle flying across the sky announces the closing of this series, and the imminence of the three remaining trumpets and their woes.

(b) *The Fifth and Sixth Trumpets* (ix. 1-21).—The next two trumpets herald forth further symbolism even more disconcerting to modern taste. Though the contents of these two visions are totally diverse in this sense, that the first is the spiritual counterpart of the other, yet so close is that alliance that I relate them in close succession, and try to explain the two together. They amount to this—that not only inanimate nature becomes God's scourge, but spirits and men may do so too. Yet not for that is the world either converted or destroyed.

The seer beholds a star fallen out of the sky lying on the earth. To it—to him we shall henceforth say—is given the key of the shaft of the abyss. He unlocks its lid, a smoke like that of a great chimney arises, darkening sky and sun. And from the smoke crawls out a swarm of locusts, which yet are more than locusts, for they sting like scorpions. These hurt, not inanimate nature any more, but men, though such only as have not God's seal upon their forehead. And even those whom they attack they may not kill, but only sting and torture as scorpions do, not necessarily to death. And these locusts, they advance like a troop of horse; but they are frightful beyond earth's cavalry. Their manes float wide like women's hair, their teeth are like lions', they are caparisoned with gold, they wear mail armour, the whir of their wings is like the roar of battle-chariot wheels, and with all this their faces are horribly human.

Their king is the Angel of the Abyss; his name in Hebrew is Abaddon, and in Greek Apolluôn, Destroyer.

Under their onslaught men seek death and find it not, and ask to die and death flees from them.

Forthwith a voice from the corners of the altar of incense, whence the saints' prayers are still ascending, bids the four angels of the Euphrates loose the winds they have held captive for so long, till the destined year and month, day and hour, should be come. And the winds are loosed.

An army of two hundred million horse advances; the riders wear cuirasses of the hue of fire and sulphur, smoke and brimstone; and fire and brimstone are breathed from the lion-jaws of their horses. And these horses, too, sting with their tails—serpent-headed tails; and with these stings and with the fire of their mouths they slay the third part of mankind. The rest were not slain, yet even so they did not repent of their idolatry, nor cease to adore their gods and their "images of gold and silver and bronze and stone and wood, that cannot see, nor hear, nor go", and they did not repent of their sorceries and wantonnesses and their thievings.

In this section I would like to show how, I feel, St. John's constructive imagination may have worked. No one can designate with any certainty the movements and reactions of another man's mind; still, we may find hints of the process. Once that is understood, we see, with at least some probability, why, at each given moment, he has reached a certain point.[1]

I do not think anyone really disputes that in the vision of the fifth trumpet John sees an invasion of evil spirits into the world, and in that of the sixth the ever-threatened invasion of the Parthians from across the Euphrates into the Roman Empire. That was, so to say, the haunting eastern peril of his time. Behind this are contemplated, of

---

[1] What was said on p. 10 about the real supernatural character of John's visions must, too, be recalled.

course, all irruptive forces such as can destroy a sick society at any period of history, and again, the eternal working out, by sin, of that doom which is God's judgment. There is, however, the brief prologue of the abyss and its angel. This needs a word.

The abyss was a familiar conception. The Hebrews had always pictured the first stage, so to call it, in creation as a chaotic mass of waters—*Tehôm*, abyss, as our version translates it (Gen. i. 2). This, under the creative influence of God's Spirit, was separated into two masses, one thrust down beneath the surface of the solid earth, the other heaved up above the solid vault of the firmament in which the stars were fixed.[1] Connected with these underground waters by association of ideas rather than by strict identification, was Sheol, the abode of departed souls—a land of silence, darkness, disorder, dust, and dismay. Job is full of this melancholy vision; Paul uses it in Rom. x. 7 concerning Our Lord's sojourn among the departed; in Luke viii. 31, evil spirits regard it as their proper place; and throughout the Apocalypse it is, simply, the place of these evil spirits—a fiery prison within the earth, to which entrance is by a well-shaft with a padlocked lid, of which the key is here entrusted to the fallen star Lucifer, the Light-Bringer, now King of Darkness, Satan (Isa. xiv. 12; Luke xi. 18). Apocalyptic literature, Enoch especially, shows that by St. John's time this notion of the abyss was well developed, though the name Abaddon is used, it appears, but rarely, and means destruction generally, or the relegation of the soul to Sheol. In the Talmud we find Abbaddon personfied.

John, therefore, sees hell's chimney opened: its smoke pours out, and with the smoke, myriads of evil spirits, like

[1] It is thus clear why, when at the last day the firmament is conceived as fallen to ruins, the stars also are cast down.

—well, flies he might have said, especially as Beelzebub,
Lord of Flies, was a name for the devil. But the plague of
locusts was described in Exodus at much greater length
than that of flies, and it follows immediately on that of the
fire and hail and storm. So locusts came quite naturally
into his mind. Possibly, too, he had seen and been impressed by a plague of locusts. Anyhow, these swarming
spirits are visualized by him as crawling, fluttering locusts.
Here, then, is one fixed topic for him, as it were, to em-
broider. But then, they are hell-locusts; they hurt worse
than locusts do. They venomously sting—they are like
scorpions. And scorpions become a second subject, con-
tributing its appropriate element of imagery. Finally, if we
are right in thinking that he already knows that this vision
is the spiritual counterpart to a Parthian invasion, what is
inseparable in imagination from the Parthians will be all
the while acting backwards into this vision, and will supply,
too, some elements for an imagery diabolically amplified—
the Parthians, proverbial for their cavalry, their floating
womanish hair, their trick of shooting poisoned arrows
backwards over their shoulder.

The advance, then, of these locusts is like a cavalry
advance—this is scarcely an exaggeration, as those who
have seen a really bad plague of locusts assure us; besides,
Joel, whom John here is almost quoting, had already compared a locust-plague, most vividly, to a cavalry advance.[1]
Well, then, these locusts are caparisoned for the fight; they
wear golden wreaths—it might be rash were we to assert
what property of locusts, armed war-horses, or Parthians,
if any, suggested this—but assuredly the locust's antennæ,
the horses' manes, and the Parthians' floating hair, meet in

[1] Also, antiquity itself had traced an odd likeness between a locust's
head and a horse's; we are told that German and Italian words for
"locusts" are *Heupferd* and *cavalletta* respectively.

the detail of the "women's hair"; and the lions' teeth come straight from Joel; and Joel, too, though no hint was necessary for this, likened the whir of the locusts' advance to that of chariot wheels. Finally, the horny "plated" body of the locust suggests the armoured cuirass, unless, indeed, that sort of detail is just the natural following out of a description of an animal prepared for a fight. And finally, the poisonous character of these locusts has already suggested "scorpions", and this, coupled with the Parthian habit of shooting poisoned arrows backwards over their shoulder, suffices to account for the "sting" in these locusts' *tails*. And all the while these horrible creatures (for, notice, here horse and rider are combined under one image; not so, of course, below) are somehow human to behold.[1]

---

[1] I must here add that the whole of this mental process, accounting for St. John's creative artistry in this section, can hold good even if his imagination had been stimulated in the way I shall now indicate, helping myself chiefly by facts adduced in Père Allo's notes on this passage. They derive much extra solidity from other notes of his bearing on the astronomical symbolism of the Apocalypse, to which, partly for lack of space, partly because I do not wish to overburden this little book with recondite mythological references and names, I scarcely allude. I will only say, however, that Père Allo seems to me at least to have shown us in what sense such allusions may be detected in St. John's book, and how astronomical and other symbolisms, embedded in or utilized by pagan myth or worship, may have affected the seer's *imagination* so as to leave their traces in his writing without our having to say even once that he used pagan myth or worship as a *source* for anything he says; and most certainly without his transporting any idea whatsoever from that pagan world whose plastic forms he was all day *seeing*, into the message he was *telling*. Job, for example, can allude to the great sea-monster, the primeval dragon living in the underground waters, Tiâmât, the ancient personification of the watery chaotic abyss, much as we could say, "That was a titanic effort", or, "The idea sprang straight from his brain like Athênê from the skull of Zeus", without either his or our admitting in the least any belief in Tiâmât, Athênê, Zeus, or Titans, or even being very conscious that we were entertaining mental images that had pagan sources at all. Take the opposite. M. Cumont alludes to "the vespers of Isis" and the "socialism of Diocletian" far more consciously, though he makes it clear that he does not suppose that the evening service in a temple of Isis was really like our Vespers, or that Diocletian's economic system was at all "socialist". But the modern facts,

At the sound of the sixth trumpet we pass definitely to the human event of which the locusts signified the spiritual counterpart, though it were still more complete to say that the Parthians themselves are only the symbol for those "God's scourges" which to the end of time shall flagellate an evil and decadent society. But just as the hell-horses are half-human, so too the human horse and rider are half-hellish; their armour has the colours of hell, and their very horses breathe forth flame, though this metaphor is by no means uncommon in Hebrew literature, or indeed in any literature. And, lest in any way these horses seem less terrible than their model, they too wound with their tails—tails, therefore, which are snake-like—tails, then, which have fangs and therefore heads. Thus does the level of the picture shift, by the rapid interpenetration of the various mental contents, from the level where human details are just

---

beneath his eyes, give him a sufficient suggestion to enable him so to speak at once naturally and without committing himself to any alien idea.

Men-scorpions and men-horses, then, were common in Babylonian imagery, and these centaurs have scorpions' tails. In the Hellenistic-Roman period this composite figure had also passed to Egypt, and stood as symbol for the zodiacal sign Sagittarius, or Archer. ... It further appears that in Hellenistic calendars locusts appear in the zodiacal sign of the Scorpion, and since from then to the end of the year there are five months, it may be that St. John's "five months", a reckoning found only here in the Apocalypse, imply that this "plague" is to last till the end of the symbolical year of the world's endurance. I add that Sagittarius was known as "diadem-wearer", and represented very often with long hair, and so in an ancient treatise are centaurs described. More might be said, as, for example, that St. John, when translating the name Abaddon by the Greek Apolluôn (Destroyer), was mentally half aware, or even fully, of the assonance between this word and Apollôn—he, too, pre-eminently an archer, whose arrows poisoned those whom they struck with plague. Enough, then, to say that complete figures of the sort St. John describes, and others (men-ants), were very common at his period and familiar to him and to everyone else, and that as Ezekiel used the Babylonian Kirubi as plastic models for his cherubs, so John, aware of it or not, may have used these other strange shapes; or, as I should prefer to say, found it easy, owing to his familiarity with such forms, for his mind, working along the lines I have described above, to terminate in the images he describes, and not to reject them as grotesque.

exaggerated or idealized, into the formally symbolical, and a Chimæra gallops forward in place of the Parthian horse.

The growth of this passage, then, seems to me not difficult to plot out, if we will but remember that John has in his mind three radiating foci of images—locust, scorpion, and Parthian cavalry; and that each shoots its peculiar rays on to and into the other, and that the combined result was made quite easy for him to retain and relate, and for his readers to accept, owing to innumerable somewhat similar plastic forms everywhere surrounding them. It is a tremulous interplay of the mental contents; not a scientific working out of one topic, of one motif, at a time, to be laid aside when done with.[1]

But for all this men are not converted; they loathe their life, they perish in great numbers, but even God's scourge, that their own action brings thus to fall on their own shoulders, will not achieve for them their salvation.

(c) *A double vision* (x., xi. 1-14).—Between the group of the fifth and sixth seals and the seventh a double vision was interposed. So here between the fifth and sixth and the seventh trumpets. Why John arranged his material in this pattern I can form no conjecture.[2] That he did so is clear; there will be other instances, and there have been small indications of the three-four grouping even where I have not mentioned them.

---

[1] In fact, a very simple parallel could be worked out with the help of Wagner's use of musical motifs. He associates—and you can often see *why* he associates—certain musical phrases with certain ideas or persons. When the persons interact, when the ideas fuse, so do the musical phrases. When the idea is modified, inverted, caricatured, so is the original music.

[2] I have since remembered that in Gen. i. (to which St. John certainly looks back in the prologue to his Gospel), after the majestic introductory sentences, the first four of the seven days form a definite group; so do the next two; and the seventh day stands by itself—a day of silence devoid of work. Indeed, the creation of plants and animals might be grouped; and then, before the seventh day, comes the twofold creation of the human race. Perhaps far-fetched.

These two parts of the "intercalated vision" are the more interesting, for not only are they to be read in close interconnection, but they look definitely forward to the second part of the book, and offer a very clear instance of John's method of dovetailing the following part of his revelation into the preceding.

I cannot tell whether he intended to symbolize thereby what in any case is true, that his visions are continually the presentments of a selfsame thing seen in a different perspective, and that what he relates consecutively is none the less in itself simultaneous.

John sees a "strong angel", who descends from heaven and plants his feet—his legs are like flashing bronze—on earth and sea; clouds encompass him, his face shines sunlike, the rainbow crowns him. In his hand he holds a "small book".

We have said that of spiritual perceptions some form themselves less by direct spiritual intuitions, clothing themselves later in such symbolism as is alone available, than by the shock of sight or sound first received and then spiritually interpreted. We do not think that happened here; but there can be no difficulty in supposing that John had very ready to his mind material supplied by the superb natural phenomena of the Ægean sea and sky. We have had instances of that already. How easily, then, thrilled by the magnificent columns of sunlight, divergent and splendidly basing themselves on a sea like molten gold and on a shore transfigured from beneath massed storm clouds through which, higher still, the haloed sun breaks forth, St. John might have drawn images under which to describe his angel. At least this softens for ourselves some of those details which are so intolerably materialized and even emphasized, say, by a Dürer.

And we know by experience garnered in almost any age

that precisely in such circumstances, under the thrilling spell of light, poets have been inspired to write, not of the light alone, but of some more spiritual world into which the light offers them access.

The angel cries with a loud voice, and the "seven thunders" utter their own. Strange event. John is preparing to write down the meaning of those voices of the Lord, when he is forbidden. There is no time for that. The angel lifts his right hand to heaven, and swears by Him who lives to the ages of the ages, who created earth and sky and sea and all things that are in them, that there shall be no more delay, but that when the seventh angel shall have sounded his trumpet, the Mystery of God shall have been accomplished, even that Gospel that He gave to His servants the Prophets to forthtell. But first, John is told, by the heavenly voice that spoke at the first with him, to take from the hand of the angel the little book, and to eat it up —not merely to read it, nor at once to announce its contents, but to assimilate it to the full and taste the mingled sweetness and bitterness of the divine communications it contained. This mandate John obeyed, and was forthwith told that he would have to prophesy once more to nations and peoples and tongues and many kings.

This angel must be seen as a pendant of that other "strong angel", who cried with a loud voice to know who should open and read the scroll that contained the whole world's history and meaning. That scroll was, in fact, opened, and in heavenly symbol all its contents were displayed. Then, at the voice of the seven trumpets, in earthly symbol, the working out of that enigma was shown. But before the seventh trumpet has sounded—and we are told quite clearly that its sounding brings us to the End—John is shown a little book, which he must master, and then prophesy again to nations and *kings*. We must see that this

lesser book contains, as it were, the elaboration of part of
what is contained in the universal scroll; or, rather, the
working out of the general law in a particular part of
history. John must announce this in its turn, and we are
given quite clearly to understand that these new prophecies are not to be accomplished *after* the sounding of the
seventh trumpet—for there is to be no more delay, such as
was spoken of to the souls beneath the altar; but upon the
sounding of that trumpet the Mystery of God was accomplished—and we need not go outside the Pauline meaning
of that word; it signifies the summing up of all things into
Christ, the triumph of God, and the salvation of the elect.

This is, in fact, shown at the end of Chapter XI, and
then St. John proceeds to relate, in two more groups of
seven, the working out of God's judgments, not in universal history this time, but strictly in the contemporary
Roman Empire, with, need I say, eternal issues at the back
of the temporal events. And the Roman Empire is that on
which his eyes are fixed from Chapter XII to the end of the
Apocalypse. Thus, once more, not only are you disembar-
rassed of the theories of those who, seeing that John seems
to have finished his prophecy, yet begins again for another
half of his book to pile vision upon vision, think he merely
stitched together documents either by himself or from
alien hands, but you are able to admire the literary precis-
ion of his work, and again, you see his mental method, so
to call it. That is, he sees all that is in, as it were, concentric
spheres—either God at the very centre of all things, then
the skyey realm of spiritual counterpart to the next realm
of history at large, then that general history itself, till the
most superficial of all is reached—contemporary happenings; or, if you prefer it, he starts with God at the outer-
most—and, indeed, penetrating all planes of existence;
then he sees the realm of everlasting truths and created, but

spiritual, existences; then the whole duration of the world; then that tiny grain of matter, so to call it, the men and things of today, at the centre of the whole.

He goes on at once to narrate in extreme abbreviation, partly under symbols he will develop at great length in ensuing chapters, the vision of which the angel spoke to him; and only then will he tell of the sounding of the seventh trumpet, and conclude this first half of his book.

In this narrative John tells how he is bidden to measure the temple and the altar and reckon up the worshippers. He is told to neglect the outer court—it is given over to the heathen to trample under foot for the space of forty-two months. For same period Christ's two witnesses, wearing sackcloth, should prophesy. (These, John adds, are the two olive-trees, or the two lamps, that stand before the face of the Lord of the Earth.) The fire of their word scorches all who would wrong them and devours their enemies. They have power over the elements during that time to dry up the rain, to turn water-springs to blood, and to scourge the earth at will. After that the Wild Beast from the abyss makes war on them and kills them, and their corpses lie in the streets of the Great City, which is called, mystically, "Sodom" and "Egypt", "where also their Lord was crucified". And men from all the peoples and tribes and tongues and races come to stare at their bodies, three days and a half, and refuse to allow their burial, and give each other gifts in their relief that the tormenting voice is silent. But after three days and a half the breath returns into them from God, they revive and stand up, and panic falls on all who see it. A voice from heaven calls them: they ascend; their enemies watch them. An earthquake ruins a tenth part of the city; seven thousand of its inhabitants perish; the rest are converted.

First of all, what are the literary elements that John is

using? Undoubtedly, the endlessly elaborate measurements of the "New Jerusalem" made for Ezekiel (xl.) by the Man whose appearance was bright like brass and his measuring rod six cubits long. Defilements were to be cast out, and God's glory was to dwell there. The altar, too, was to be measured, and the ritual was prescribed (xliii. 13-17). And again, Zechariah (ii.) sees the "man", or angel, with the measuring line go to define the New Jerusalem.

Further, John uses, here and often in the second part of his book, the number which had become quite recognized as "persecution-time"—the space during which the Jews suffered under Antiochus Epiphanes, June, 168, to December, 165 B.C., as told by Daniel (vii. 25, etc.). This was, in apocalyptic phrasing, "a time, times, and half a time", three years and a half, or forty-two months, or 1,260 days.

Again, he recalls the passage in Zech. iv. where the elect people is the lamp, fed by the streams of oil pouring from the two olive-trees, who "stand before the Lord of the whole earth". Probably, in Zechariah, these represent Joshua and Zerubbabel, the heads of the priesthood and of the royal house respectively. Also, John is not forgetful of the traditional portrait of Elijah, who was to return before the Day of Yahweh (Mal. iv. 5-6); he brought down fire upon God's enemies, and Sirach (xlviii. 1) saw him "stand up like fire, and his word was on fire like a lamp"; he, too, was famous for his "shutting up" the heavens (3 (1) Kings xvii. 1), and in Luke (iv. 25, cf. James v. 17) the drought lasted three and a half years, equated thus with the Syrian domination of Antiochus. During the Transfiguration, with Elijah was associated Moses, and it is Moses whom St. John's plagues recall; but in popular tradition it was Enoch who was coupled with Elijah (see 4 Esdras vi. 26), as being not yet dead, but to reappear at the end.

Finally, the image supremely proper to the next great section of the book, the Wild Beast, enters this résumé of the story that next section will narrate; John speaks of him as "the" Wild Beast, as though he had been already mentioned; but no; in the previous vision, where the abyss had been seen, no beast had been disgorged from it, but the king of its spirits, not thus described. Just as the Parthian imagery shot itself backwards into the vision of the locusts, so here—the Beast, and the New Jerusalem.

These then, I think, are the sources from which John's symbols flow into his mind. What, now, is their meaning here?

John is describing the Church in the midst of persecutions—in the foreground, the Roman persecutions; further back in the perspective, those in which the Church lives to the end of time, her continual apparent defeat and destruction, and her glorious ultimate triumph.

John shows, then, the Church under the figure of the whole Temple with its outer courts; but only the Temple proper is measured and defined; that much is to be kept intact, undefiled, occupied by the faithful till the end. The rest is to be invaded and trampled under foot by the rebels and the unregenerate like so many wild beasts. But God never leaves Himself without a witness, and throughout this very time His two witnesses are preaching outside the sacred and inviolate enclosure, and are in continual conflict with the enemies of God. There will be a moment when they seem quite conquered by the Wild Beast, who incarnates in himself, as it were, the uttermost of evil; but their apparent death shall be to the period of their witness as no more than three days and a half to three years and a half; after that, it will be seen that God's witness is not irrevocably slain, but that the indestructible Church is, at the last, triumphant.

In the history of the world shall be, then, recurrently, a

nucleus of faithful; a prolonged missionary effort in a world determined to have none of Christ; brief periods when it seems that her voice has been for ever silenced, and her constant resurrection from the dead, and her final exaltaton.

A few details ought to be added. Why, if the immediate fact in John's mind is the Roman persecution, is this scene placed at Jerusalem, and not rather, for example, at Babylon, the "cipher" name for Rome, quite definitely, at this time? Presumably because, having started to think in terms of temple and two witnesses and much more that was purely Old Testament in origin, he found the scene placed for him, so to say, in Jerusalem, and worked the story out there. Besides, Jerusalem was, alas! the great apostate, and though Christ was everywhere crucified in the person of His faithful, it was in Jerusalem that the historical crucifixion had occurred. Besides, it was in Jerusalem that the "abomination that maketh desolate" had been set up—the image of Zeus in the Holy of Holies, by Antiochus. And John's mind, if only because of the Daniel-number 1,260 and its equivalents, could not but have in its explicit memory the desecration of that crisis in his nation's history. It has, too, been asked whether there was no tradition of a definitely Jewish Antichrist, who should rise in the Holy City. It is quite possible; and in the Antichrist prophecy of 2 Thess. ii. the Son of Perdition takes his seat in the Temple.

I would finally ask why St. John, wishing to describe the constant witness of the Church in a sinful world, does so under the image of *two* witnesses. First, his use of Ezekiel's picture of the measurement of the Temple sends his thought to Zechariah's measurement scene, and thence to that prophet's symbol of the two olive-trees; add to this the tremendously strong, though varied, belief in the apparition of Two on the eve of the great day of Yahweh;

and, finally, the fact that in Jewish law two witnesses were required to give valid sanction to what they said. There is no Christian tradition as to any particular personalities here involved. I should not wonder if Peter and Paul were not somewhere in St. John's mind. Since Zechariah's two olive-trees are the heads of ecclesiastical and lay categories respectively, I wonder that undivided Christendom did not see in them the Pope and Emperor, except that the extinction of these, even temporarily, would have seemed a blasphemous surmise. It remains that we are fully permitted to see in them what we have said, and such today is, I think, the general view.

John's attention therefore oscillates to and fro between the near and the far perspective. Close at hand he sees the Empire, and more widely the recurrent persecutions hurling themselves against the witness that the Church ever opposes to an anti-Christian world; widest of all, the unceasing conflict of the spirit of Christ and of Antichrist. The Church shrinks back upon herself; is narrowed down to her ramparted refuge of doctrine and of worship—on her defensive in a world that should have been all holy-city, all holy-land, but tends ever to become the unholiest of cities (Sodom), the sinfullest of lands (Egypt); nay, one huge Calvary upon which all the while Christ is recrucified. From that one faithless town which nailed Jesus to His cross John's eye roves to Rome, whither St. Peter had seen Christ travel to be slain, in His martyrs, once again, and thence to the whole angry, murderous world. Then returning, after the hour of silenced voice, of catacomb existence, he sees revival—moral and social shock sets the world to tremble, obstinate perversity destroys in its despair a portion of the old order; not its majority, one would say, since but a tenth of the city falls, and the remainder, fear-converted, worship God.

A doubtful, hesitating issue, yet a true psychological estimate, accurately verified by experience, of all history short of that universal, consummated history in which the new and for ever pure Jerusalem is established and shall not fall away.

(*d*) *The seventh trumpet* (xi. 15-18).—After the breaking of the seventh seal there was silence. Here there is acclamation. But what does John see? I do not think he sees anything. For I feel bound to link the vision of the Ark to the scenes that follow. This is but to follow a plan dating as far back as the famous commentary of Andreas of Cæsarea in the Eastern Church (fifth or sixth century), and as Albertus Magnus (1260) in the West. Not only is it essentially suitable that the "third woe" should not be in any way described (it is the same thing as the seventh trumpet) any more than the seventh seal was; but verse 19 is peculiarly appropriate as the preface to the second part of the book, while ascriptions such as are read in xi. 16-18 habitually close their section.

Therefore, after the sounding of the trumpet, great voices are heard to cry out:

There has come to pass
The Kingdom over the world of Our Lord and of His Christ,
    And He shall reign for the ages of the ages.

Upon these voices—of angels, or of the four?—those of the four-and-twenty elders break in:

We give Thee thanks, O Lord, God the All-Governor,
    Who ART and who WAST,[1]

---

[1] Notice this phrase. "Who Art to Come" is *not inserted*. For He *is* come. The seventh trumpet marks the end of the world. All the more clearly do we see that what follows in the *book* is not meant as following in *time*. It is the elaboration in terms of contemporary history, first and foremost, of what has been already related in more general terms in previous chapters.

Because Thou hast assumed Thy power, Thy great power,
And hast begun to reign.
The heathen were full of wrath,
But the wrath of Thyself did come,
And the hour for the dead to be judged,
And for giving their wage to Thy servants the Prophets,
And to the saints and to them that fear Thy name,
The small and the great,
And for destroying those that do destroy the earth.

Thus, then, closes the first part of the Apocalypse. Let us summarize the visions St. John has seen:

First, he has been made aware of God, the Ultimate, the Eternal, the Absolute Majesty.

Then he has seen that God is, as it were, ringed by circle upon circle of created reality—by spirits, by men, and by "inanimate" nature; and that these *many* yet make *one* universe, vocal with one harmony of praise.

And yet, that that very world is an enigma, insoluble save by Him who, being God, yet died, and again lives triumphant, a sacrifice eternally accepted and life-giving.

Such is, reduced as it were to its ultimate, simplest, most enduring elements, the whole history of Creation.

But the *parts* of the enigma are forthwith displayed, not yet in the concrete instance, nor seen in time and place, but as enduring laws, so to say, that shall express themselves in all times and places. The created world tries to constitute itself into a self-sufficient empire or cosmos. Idle hope? Ever does such an effort issue into war, or into an evil and inhuman peace, and into ruin. Yet within even such chaos-cosmos are souls who rise superior to it, die rather than yield to it, and triumph in this dying, till at last the number is completed and the total Church full-formed, and the rival would-be-eternal world-empire crashes to its end (iv.-viii. 1).

Then comes the consummation, of which no human tongue can speak.

John now focusses his eye more nearly on the concrete, on these general laws working themselves out, but still in *general* history. In his double prefatory vision the spiritual Godward effort is seen returning on itself, as it were, and having its effect upon the earth (viii. 2-5). Constantly God's "plagues" chastise the world, though without destroying it; yet men are not converted. Even human scourges, even the God-hating spirits who inspire them, are *God's* scourges. At no time does God permit His witness in the world to disappear, the authentic interpretation of Himself to be utterly silenced. Even when at moments the prophetic voice seems stilled it will revive once more, and the worst defeat of God is but the preface to His final triumph. But of that final triumph, once more, John cannot tell us.

Has, then, this part of the Apocalypse told us much, we may dare to ask, that we did not in some sense know already? We knew that behind all else God exists. We knew that in all His creation He is operative. And again that He has His court; that ten thousand times ten thousand spirits do Him service and find therein their joy. And we knew, alas! that in the world He made there are evil wills that resist Him—wills of fallen angels and wills of men. And our faith teaches, what reason cannot doubt, that God in the end shall conquer.

And our faith teaches, too, that the eternal Son of God became Man for our redemption, suffered, died, rose again, and triumphed too, and that we, if we be faithful to Him, shall triumph, even though, time after time, we, His Church, appear to have been defeated.

Has John told us much more than this?

I shall not here in any way comment on his strange, yet magnificent and immortal, imagery, nor on the enthralling rhythm of his words. Through these, but not because of them, the ineffaceable impression of his book is made.

I feel that just because the book is an inspired book, that it has had God for its Author, it drives deep into us what we knew already, but held, perhaps, less convincedly. It gives us, so that we can assimilate it, identify it with ourselves, that simple yet tremendous instruction that we have recapitulated; it makes us *worship* what we know; it persuades us towards that consciousness, which is so valuable, of the universal adoration, given by angels and men and nature to Him who sits upon the throne of eternity, and dwells in light inaccessible. If our worship, and our recognition of what we have seen, expresses itself best in silence, what matter? In heaven itself that silence is to be found, when word and symbol fail.

But, also, because in many ways we have seen how human is the book, how wholly John's, how proper to his world and place and time, how full of human suffering, love and fear; have seen what is its pathos, its intimate innumerable links with our experiences—we feel it is not a thing belonging to a distant past, for scholars to study or for saints only to muse upon. It cannot but be a possession for ourselves. An encouragement, a constant food for hope. And all the more will it be so when John, having plunged us, as he will, far deeper into the problems of his own immediate age, lifts us, at the very end, not merely back to universal history, but to the consummation of all history, and to a world united, in ways beyond all nature's hope, to the Most Blessed Trinity.

Meanwhile the fight remains. The end is not yet. In our time as in his, the world, visible and invisible, is a vast battlefield. Woe to us if we forget it; but folly in us if we fear. Not only shall God's elect go unscathed, in their inmost self, from the disasters of this world, but notice, those very disasters, which are the Judgment of God, are the working-out of sin. It is *wrong-doing* that issues into war, and famines, and sickness, and revolution, and death. In a true sense, man condemns and punishes himself. Yet even though we be conscious of sin in ourselves, and tremble lest we perish, even so the great opposing forces clash, not in us alone, nor even first, but in the person of the Incarnate Christ; and though for a space, in Himself and in us, He be outspread on the rack of the Cross, the Cross is not the end, any more than our conflict is, but resurrection and everlasting reign. For Him, that *must* be; for us, if we choose, it ever may be.

Part B1

This part of the Apocalypse is prefaced by a vision of the heavenly temple opened, and approach is offered to all, to come in even to the Ark of the Covenant, once hidden, now revealed with its full significance of an eternal alliance made between God and the world, and the chosen place on which the presence of His glory rests. If, indeed, this brief vision be properly placed thus at the head of this second part, it is parallel with the vision of Christ moving about in His Church; here again, Christ in His Church is no less vividly portrayed. And it is with that Church, still on earth, that the remainder of the book directly deals (xi. 19).

I. (i) A Double Prefatory Vision (xii. 1-17)

In clear parallelism with the double vision of the worship of the heavenly court, and of the role in human history of God made flesh, is seen now a double vision too—the Mother of Christ, and the Dragon. It is *announced* as a symbol—a "sign" or token; and like the initial visions on each occasion, is in the sky.

(*a*) There is shown, then, in the sky, a woman, clothed with the sun, the moon under her feet, her head crowned with twelve stars. She is in travail and cries aloud with her pain. She is confronted by a dragon, fiery-red, with seven heads crowned royally, and ten horns. His lashing tail sweeps from their places one-third of the stars of heaven. He waits to see her delivered of her child, that he may devour it. The child is born, a male, and is caught away to the throne of God, thence to rule the world with a Messianic sceptre.

(*b*) The Dragon makes a mad attack on Him, but Michael and his angels withstand him; the angel armies clash, there is war in the sky, and the Dragon is cast head-long, and his angels with him. As for the Woman, she "fled to the desert, where she has a place prepared for her by God, and there they tend her for 1,260 days."

A voice cries:

Now hath come to pass
The salvation and the power and the kingdom of our God,
And the dominion of His Christ,
Because the accuser of our brethren is cast down,
He who accuses them before our God night and day.
And they did conquer him
Because of the blood of the Lamb and the word of their witness,
And they loved not their life, even unto dying.
Therefore, exult, ye heavens, and ye who tabernacle therein,
And woe to the earth and the sea,
Because the devil hath come down to you with a fierce heart,
For he knows that the time he hath is brief.

This vision is, as it were, a rapid sketch of all that will follow, save the *final* triumph. John has indicated, in lightning-flash words, all the symbols that he will use here-after, or rather, he will do little else than develop and apply them in detail. What, then, do they mean? Let us start with what is quite certain.

The Child is Christ; the Woman is His Mother; and the Dragon is Satan, and with him all the powers of evil. That the Child is the Messiah none can doubt. The angelic hymn makes that clear, were it not so in any case. The Devil over Him, at any rate, has no power. He is caught up to God's throne, intangible, and the Messianic iron-shod shepherd's staff is placed in His hand.

His Mother, then? To many, accustomed to a certain symbolism proper to devotional art, it may come as a shock if we say: Not, at least directly, Our Blessed Lady. Here, at least, tradition is very full and helpful. She is the Universal Church, whose travail gave birth to the Messiah. Victorinus,[1] who of the Latins was the first to comment on the Apocalypse, declared:

> She is the ancient Church of the patriarchs and the prophets, and the saints and the apostles. The groanings and the torments of her yearning were upon her until she should see that Christ, the fruit of her people according to the flesh, promised to her long since, had from that very race taken up a body.

And St. Hippolytus, who died after 235, and wrote in Greek,[2] saw in the Woman that Church which ceaselessly bears sons to God. "Even", adds Beatus (776), "was this Woman, before the Lord's advent, in travail", and so Augustine. Idle to pile up witnesses: if divergences there be, they regard chiefly the point, Is the Church here spoken of the ancient Jewish Church, the Synagogue, or both that Church *and* the Church that Christ has founded? Without any doubt it is both; the universal Mother of Christ, who,

---

[1] Died under Diocletian.
[2] Though his commentary is lost, from other works of his we know some of his ideas on particular points.

in other imagery, may be described as His Spouse. "Never", cries Hippolytus, "shall the Church cease producing from her heart the Word that, in the world, is persecuted by the unbelieving." "Ever", wrote St. Bede, "the Church, though the Dragon fight against her, is bearing Christ."

But does this mean that St. John was not thinking of Mary, too? Impossible that he should not so have thought of her. Who, knowing that Jesus had been born of Mary, could have failed, when speaking of His Mother, to have found his thoughts straying to her? Not St. John, assuredly, who for so long had tended Mary and interwoven her life with his. "From that hour he took her to his own." Once more, what is true on one level is true, in such matters as these, on all. And John, as we shall see, has yet a third level for his awareness. The Woman is the second and predestined Eve.

Whence does John draw the symbolism of her raiment? Sion, indeed, had been, in the Old Testament, continually portrayed as a woman, and from Jewish tradition the figure had reached Christian literature. Especially noteworthy is St. Paul's allegorical reference to the "Jerusalem on high that is the mother of us all" (Gal. iv. 26, and Heb. xi. 10, xii. 22, etc.). And from early times the spouse in the Canticle had been interpreted of her. There she was seen coming forth as the dawn, fair as the moon, and exquisite as sunlight: and in the Testament of the Twelve Patriarchs, the two chiefs, Levi and Judah, had been likened to sun and moon, and between, beneath Judah's feet, twelve rays were seen.

And the Dragon? For the moment let us seek no detailed explanation of his heads, his horns, and his diadems. The seven heads are here not likely to mean more than a plenitude of such powers as are his, or are conceived in hideous travesty of the other "sevens" already noted, especially the Seven Spirits of God. And in view of the great use John is about to make of a vision in Daniel, the ten horns are scarcely to be sought from elsewhere than that prophecy. But in a moment John describes this Dragon as that primeval serpent—that is, Satan and the Slanderer—whose role it is to accuse before God those whom he wishes to wrest from the divine hands. Here, then, John's mind has gone back to the Book of Genesis, and that is why we can be sure that in his contemplation of the Woman the thought of Eve was present. Satan, the serpent of Genesis, the eternal adversary, a murderer from the beginning (John viii. 44); a liar and seducer of that world which, he declares, is given wholly over to him (Luke iv. 6), and of which he is the lord (John xvi. 11; cf. xiv. 30, xii. 31). And in the sweep of his tail he carries away with him the third of the stars that give light to the world.[1]

We see, then, a rich and manifold vision of, you may say, all existence, "all creation groaning and travailing together", till Christ be revealed; the universal Eve, before whom the Adversary of mankind is ever on the watch; the Elect People, the mystical Israel of God; the immortal Mother of the Messiah, on whom no less immortal a perse-

[1] I wish not to enter into the complicated question of astronomical or mythological elements, literary or artistic, which might have been used by St. John in this description. He might have made such use, had he wished; or, unconsciously, the Oriental imagery to which he was, or could have been, accustomed, seeing that it was everywhere around him, could have influenced his pictorial imagination. But it is quite easy to derive every element of his picture from Jewish sources, and there is no call to go farther afield. In no case will he have carried across with them any of the ideas which that imagery conveyed to a pagan. If I had to indicate one pagan art motif rather than another, it would be the Gigantomachia, or conflict of Zeus with the Giants, figured on that altar at Pergamum which he surely saw as the "Throne of Satan". The Giants who were trying to take heaven by assault would almost certainly have been portrayed with serpents' tails.

cution shall bear heavy; and, finally, Mary the Mother of
Our Lord, against whom Cæsar shall set up his impious
lordship.

But before we are told to watch the actual conflict upon
earth we see, as usual, its skyey counterpart—war in that
interspace where the "powers of the air" have their
domain. St. Paul (Eph. ii. 2, vi. 12) speaks thus. Michael,
his very name a war-cry, "Who is like unto God?" attacks
and conquers that Dragon who, none the less, we shall see,
continues to set himself up in horrible rivalry with the
Highest. But from the sky Christ sees him fall like lightning (Luke x. 18). And heaven can sing the serene triumph
of the Child, and in Him, ultimately, of His "many
brethren".[1]

The scene now passes to the earth, and a series of seven
mysteries is shown, of which the first four form a group—
the Dragon, the Wild Beast from the Sea, the Wild Beast
from the Land, and the Lamb.

But the first of these still relates, under universal
symbols, what the rest will tell of with reference to
particular persons and events.

I. (ii) SEVEN MYSTERIES

(a) A Group of Four Mysteries (xiii. 1-xv. 4)

Before the Serpent's onslaught the spiritual Eve flies,
with a swiftness that even the winged and skyey monster

[1] It has been the opinion of many theologians, formed quite independently of this passage, that it was from the outset the divine plan to achieve
the supernatural salvation of the world, even had there been no original
sin, by means of the incarnation of the Second Person of the Blessed
Trinity, into whom all things should thus be recapitulated. In the person of
the Word made flesh, all creation was to find its harmony within itself, and
between itself and God. In this way the angels would have had to reach
their destiny by subordination to One who was, in His human nature,
lower than themselves. It was this that they refused, and by so doing fell.

cannot equal, to the desert; her flight is swift as that of the
eagle, the "great" eagle, "the great-winged, the wide in his
outstretching" (Esdr. xvii. 3); the eagle on whose wings
Yahweh would carry His people (Exod. xix. 4; Deut.
xxxii. 11, etc.); and in the wilderness, away from the
tyrannical attack, she survives for the 1,260 days of persecution—the time, times, and half a time of prophecy. So
Israel in its desert; so the devout Jews hidden among their
rocks and in their caves from Antiochus; so the Holy
Family in Egypt; so, perhaps, the Jerusalem Christians
taking refuge in Pella (cf. Mark xiii. 14); so the Asiatic
Christians isolated from so much human intercourse; so
the Christians of all times, withdrawn into their holy
place, while their witnesses go forth but to preach and die.
And there in the desert they feed her on desert food, the
manna, or, as Elijah was fed, on bread that gave him
strength for forty days, or, as we are, on our better than
that bread from heaven. The Devil casts out against her
floods of persecution; turbulent torrents of water pursue
her;[1] but the earth gapes and swallows the floods, even as
the streams in the tortured Asiatic land sink into the
fissured soil and lose themselves. Back, therefore, the
Dragon turns to attack the remainder of the Woman's
seed, those who keep the commands of God and the
witness to Jesus.

This vision is transitional. That is enough to account for
what to some might seem strange—that the Devil should
turn back from attacking the Church to attack those who,
after all, are themselves the Church. Provided we keep
John's various ways of looking at the same thing in our
minds, the difficulty vanishes. The Woman is the Church;
she bears her Son—conceived from all eternity in the

---

[1] The primeval dragon lived in, and indeed *was*, the chaotic watery
abyss.

divine plan—and then innumerable other sons, His brothers. This universal motherhood has nothing to do with time; idle to ask, therefore, when these "other sons" were born, as though there had been no time for other births between the Messiah's birth and the flight. The Woman exists upon one plane of thought—the spiritual, the transcendent; and the war with the faithful is on quite another, the terrestrial plane of time. This is not so much a case of "dovetailing" of visions, as an easy passage from the general covering vision, which shows the thing in its universal symbolic form, to the departmental visions which will show the same thing in other symbols suited to the facts of daily life. To these we now turn.

John sees a wild beast coming from the sea—leopard-like for fierce swift cruelty, yet trampling like a bear, and with lion-like roar. It is seven-headed, and ten-horned, and on each horn a royal crown, and on each head blasphemous titles. One of those heads had received a mortal wound; but, though mortal, it had been healed.

To this beast the Dragon delegates his power and throne and a great authority. And the whole world goes gaping after the Beast, and bows down before the Dragon and before the Beast, chanting: "Who is like unto the Beast, and who can go to war with it?" And it begins, indeed, to speak with pride and blasphemy, and for two-and-forty months it rails against God and those over whom His heavenly tent is spread; it fights the saints and conquers them; its power stretches over the whole civilized world. All whose names had not been written from the foundation of the world, in the Lamb's Book of Life, adored him.

"Should they not fight him?" cry the despairing Christians. No! if prison be your fate, accept imprisonment, answers the exiled seer. If you take the sword, by the sword you shall also perish. Even so, O Christian, keep faith alike and patience.

Before explaining this I will relate the vision of the Wild Beast from the earth.

This second Beast shows itself as coming from the land. It had but two horns, like a lamb's, but its voice was a dragon's. It works under the eye of the first beast, and with his subdelegated authority. It causes all the inhabited earth to worship the Beast who had conquered them; it works miracles; fire descends, at its bidding, from the sky; it causes images of the Beast to be made; it gives a voice to these images ... all who refuse to worship are slain.

Rich and poor, free and slave, have to be branded with the Beast's name or number upon forehead or right hand; none, save those thus branded, can buy or sell.

"Here is the riddle for spiritual wit to solve. Reckon up the number of the Beast—for it is the number of *a man*. It is six hundred and sixty-six."

The first clear point is that John, in the picture of the first Beast, models himself on Daniel vii. Here, for once, he accumulates instead of simplifying. In Daniel the four winds strike the Mediterranean, and from it emerge successively four monsters, representing each of them a kingdom or an empire—which, we need not trouble here to specify. The first was a lioness, then came a bear; then a leopard; and finally a monster devouring, trampling, iron-fanged, ten-horned, and then producing another horn, a horn with human eyes and a mouth speaking "great"— i.e., proud and overweening—things. It devoured and threshed and broke the whole earth, and "made war upon the saints and prevailed against them", and thought to upset the very laws of life, and raged for the "time, times, and half a time" with which we are now familiar. This certainly is Antiochus Epiphanes, and the ten horns are his predecessors or rivals in the Syrian Empire. He was the first of whom the Jews had experience as requiring to be acknowledged as God made manifest.

From his island John descries the world-power of horizon-hidden Rome. This Beast is the Roman Empire. Of its heads and horns I will speak below. But it is not on these, taken one by one, that John here insists, not even on that which has been wounded to death and has recovered. But he does most certainly insist that this has been what the Beast itself has suffered, and therein sees without a doubt an insolent travesty, which he will later on elaborate, of the Lamb, slain, yet risen from its death. To Rome, Satan, in his pride for which God mocks him, has entrusted what he believes to be his throne and his world power: "They are mine," he had said of the kingdoms of this world, "and to Thee will I give them, if Thou wilt fall down and adore me." What Satan could give, the Beast had accepted, and in the pride of that power, heard the world exclaim after him: Who is like to the Beast? ignorant of immortal Michael and his battle-cry: Who is like to God?

The essence of the satanic role of the Empire was that it now demanded that itself and its Emperors should be worshipped as divine. It would be out of place here to detail the gradual rise, spread, implications, and special forms of this; enough to say that Asia was the best of any homes for the cult, slavishly flattering as she was, and well ahead of other lands in the exuberance of her homage. By now the Emperor could be called God, Son of God, Lord, Saviour, Saviour of the World, and had his "Lord's Day", his Epiphany, and his visits to a city were called *Parousia*. These names of blasphemy were what men gave to him almost perforce, even when he rejected or deprecated them himself. And the tendency was unmistakable.

Once Rome had started on this line she would never stop till, as has been said, by the time of Decius and Diocletian, the Emperor cult had practically recapitulated into itself all the religious organization of the Empire. Here again was a hateful travesty of the Christian ideal.

But the travesty was not yet complete.

John sees a second Beast, coming this time from the land—from the mainland—that is, Asia. This Beast, notice, has but a delegated power: it is the viceroy of the first Beast, even as that Beast was the viceroy of Satan. He will be called later on the false prophet. We shall see special reason for that; but here notice that this Beast is mild compared to the first—he has little horns like a lamb, though his voice is the very voice of the Dragon. Not for nothing had Our Lord said: "Beware of false prophets, that come to you in sheep's clothing, but inwardly are ravening wolves ..." Who, then, is this second Beast? There are those who would see in him the actual Asiarch of St. John's day. The Asiarch was the high-priest of the Emperor cult in each city, supreme in his own temple and group, but also the president of the entire league (*commune*) of Emperor-worship in the province of Asia. It was his business to direct the cult throughout the province and to preside at the five-yearly games. But his power was one of organization rather than command; that belonged, if to anyone, to the proconsul and to his subordinate magistrates. Before these would delinquent Christians be brought for trial, and they alone, one may suppose, could order and inflict punishments. Almost, then, I would agree that the second beast is the complete authority of that most grossly adulatory province, civil and religious combined: a collectivity comparable thus far to the symbol of the Woman, who represents the Church as opposed to the persecuting anti-Christian Empire, and to the first beast, who represents, not this Emperor or that, nor even the city Rome, but Rome as the great adversary, the would-be divine counter-claimant, God-on-earth.

How, then, would the Asiatic power express itself? I have explained how Emperor-worship entered into every part of life, and how to keep clear of it involved practical ostracism, if nothing worse. Now this cult revolved round the Emperor's statue, or his effigy or emblem of whatever sort, from the official statues in the temple to public images or busts, to the standards and even coins. It would be impossible to exaggerate the lengths to which this imperial image-worship was carried. Scarcely a human act could be carried out in presence of one of the Emperor's statues without risk of arrest, as though treason had been committed against the august majesty. In the trials of the Christian it was these statues that were to be made the ultimate test of loyalty. Pliny wrote to Trajan (*Ep.* xcvi.; A.D. 112) from Bithynia, in the north of the province, how he would produce the statue of the Emperor together with those of the gods, and command the prisoners to do homage to it with wine and incense. If they did this they were freed.

Was magic or sheer conjuring trick used in connection with this still further to impress the popular imagination? There is no evidence that I know of that this was done in connection with the Emperor cult. But it is quite certain that magic was in great repute in this period, and not least in Asia Minor. Acts xix. 19 relates the burning by Christians of the "Ephesian writings", or books of magic spells, which were widely notorious: and both the Apocalypse and St. Paul's Epistles take it for granted that magic was at least believed in and known to be very wrong. Charlatanism of all sorts was practised with wide success. Apollonius of Tyana was a contemporary of St. John, and had made Ephesus almost his headquarters. His biography describes his miracles. Even if these were a later development of his story, the shrines of the serpent-wanded Asklepios were always claiming miracles. The Emperor cult itself used symbolism, as when an eagle attached to the dead Emperor's funeral pyre and liberated by the flames was seen to soar aloft and lose itself in the sky. Other images were "miraculous". In the bas-reliefs of the Mithra-cult—a very Asiatic religion—a hideous snake-entwined figure is seen emitting flames from its mouth, and similar statues have been found equipped with tubes which would make some such phenomenon quite manageable. Or were these speaking statues? Ventriloquism, at any rate, is known to have been used for such purposes; and Alexander of Abonoteichos had a talking snake. Simon Magus, too, was everywhere believed to have claimed the power of animating statues, though that may be based on this very passage of the Apocalypse. We shall, then, be by no means rash if we suppose the miracles of the Second Beast to represent real happenings. If we hesitate to do this, we may be content to suppose that St. John means, at least, that the authorities could at any moment summon persecution as fierce as fire—a monstrous parody of Elijah's, or even of that heavenly fire which John himself had wished to see fall on the inhospitable village—to descend upon the Christians, and that the sinister voice of the omnipresent Emperor was to be heard through the lips of every one of his relentless images.

It can hardly be said that the Roman administration set out to persecute as by preference. On the contrary, it was extraordinarily tolerant, and allowed everyone to follow his own worship provided he did not exclude the official cults. Nor did anyone, except the Christians and the Jews, attempt to do so. Everyone was learning at this time to see in any one god only another form or name of all the rest. Pagans proved not unready to take over Yahweh and even Christ into their pantheons, and hyphen them, as it were, to local cults like that of Sabazios or Orpheus. It was, then, with an air of the sweetest reasonableness that they asked the Christians to be no less tolerant. What harm, the martyrs were to be asked very little later, in throwing a few grains of incense on to the burning coals and hailing Cæsar as what he most certainly was—*Kurios*, or Lord? And the letters to the Seven Churches seemed, as we saw, to show that there were not a few Christians who found a way of forming their consciences and regarding these rites as merely civic.

I am myself inclined to think that in St. John's own day the local stress amounted, at least officially, to not much more than this. There is no other evidence that a sanguinary persecution or even very harsh official measures were just now being taken. But everyone knows that unofficial persecution can be worse than public and official, and that the latter scarcely begins till a strong public opinion permits it. And St. John, quite apart from the light of prophecy, could scarcely but foresee that the day was nearing when public opinion would be all on the side of active persecution, especially as he had no illusions on the count of the Jews, who would satisfy their own hatred for the Christians, and very likely cover themselves with a mantle of vicarious orthodoxy and imperial zeal by egging on the populace to anger against the faithful, as they did in the case of St. Polycarp. He was martyred for refusing Emperor-worship, but the instigators of the arrest were the Jews. So even if we do not think the Apocalypse by itself to be evidence that a persecution was actually going on, it certainly is evidence that all the elements of persecution were there, and, indeed, that the unofficial persecution, the popular boycott, had already begun. The nonconforming Christians were already "marked men".

Was there ever a sense in which they actually were branded? What was the mark and number of the Beast that they were to receive on forehead or on hand under pain of being excluded from all citizen life?

In 217 B.C. Ptolemy I, Philopator, had caused the Jews who submitted to registration to be branded with the stamp of the worshippers of Dionysos; soldiers, slaves, and certain devotees were stamped with appropriate devices. But here I think that the Emperor's mark is again a travesty—at least in part—of the stamp or "seal" conferred in Baptism and alluded to in symbol in Chapter VII. Beast's mark is opposed to the Lamb's mark. But, says St. John, the Beast's name is a number, and the number of a man. He challenges them to reckon it out and to read his cipher.

The general principle here presents no difficulty. Both in Hebrew and in Greek letters stood for numbers. Thus *alpha* was 1, *beta* 2, *iota* 10, and so on. Therefore a proper name could be stated as a number, the sum of its letters. This was a very common performance—almost a game. An inscription scrawled on a wall at Pompeii says: "I love her whose number is 545". Even the Epistles of Barnabas and St. Irenæus (*Adv. Hær.*, II, xxiv, 1, 2) have examples; and the Sibylline Oracles (i. 324-31) say: "Then shall come among men the Son of the Great God ... having four vowels: the consonant in Him is doubled. But I will tell you the full number: Eight units, as many tens, and eight hundreds—that is what the Name shall reveal to the friends of unbelief, to men; but do thou in thy mind think upon the immortal and most high Son of God, the Christ." The name IESOUS, then, as it stood in Greek, amounted to 888. I shall revert to this number in a moment.

Whose, then, was the name 666?

To start with, Irenæus gives a variant reading, 616. He himself had already lost the key. Omitting all the fantastic interpretations offered in the course of time, which include Luther, various Popes, and others, we may ask to whom, in St. John's day, could the title of Beast be particularly applicable, now that our eyes have thus been turned to imperial Rome? Caligula has been suggested, who attempted to have his statue set up in the temple at Jerusalem, and was especially eager to have himself worshipped. His name—Gaius Cæsar—does in fact amount in Greek letters to 616. But this madman was not a notorious persecutor, and is unlikely to be thus singled out as representative by John. But Nero was an Emperor whose persecuting role was quite exceptional—we shall have much more to say about him soon—and Nero Cæsar, written in Hebrew first without the final "n" of Neron, as in Latin, and then with it as in Greek, gives first 616, and then 666.

When, then, we recall that the number of Our Lord's name could be given as 888, *one more* throughout than the "perfect number" seven, it can be easily seen that the number of Antichrist would be most appropriately, in accordance, too, with various other ideas into which we really cannot enter, *one less* than the seven-group—that is, 666. And just as the universal spirit of persecution, as it were, incarnates itself, for John, in Rome, so the eternal Antichrist has for his concrete representative the Emperor Nero. *Isopsephia* was a department of this general "game" of number-names. When you found that two names or a name and an adjective added up into the same number, or that a name was "worth" a number that already had some special significance attached to it, you concluded to a mysterious connection between the two. If, then, the special number of Antichrist was recognized as 666, and it was seen that Nero's name and title added up into the same, the connection between Nero and Antichrist would be forthwith established.

Lest these terrible pictures of dragon and of beasts overwhelm the readers, a vision follows in which the Lamb, standing on Mount Sion the immovable—not like the Dragon, on the shifting sand (xii. 18)—gathers to Himself His firstfruits, the perfect numbers, 144,000, like those who were seen in Chapter VII to form the true Israel of God.

And a new song is sung—sung, indeed, by the immortal citizens of heaven, in presence of the four and of the twenty-four, but that can be learnt by those who, ransomed from the world, on whose lips was no lie, are flawless, are virgins, and follow the Lamb whithersoever He goeth. *Expertus potest credere Quid sit Iesum diligere.*

So closes this first group of four visions, with a revelation of cheer and triumph, John's gaze shifting from the wicked city, doomed to fall, to the impregnable Acropolis of God. And round the Lamb are *His* "sealed", on whose brow is no Beast's sign, but His name and His Father's; who worshipped no lie, but knew the faith and kept it. Betrothed to God, they guarded their soul's chastity of love, unlike that harlot world that sold and sells its allegiance to all that is not God.

(b) *The Fifth and Sixth Mysteries* (xiv. 6-13)

John reinforces this picture of triumph by three angelic proclamations, which announce, first, the advent of God's judgment upon the world at large; then His judgment upon the great pagan city, now, by anticipation, called by the apocalyptic name of Babylon, and described as the world's wanton:

She fell! She fell! Babylon the Great—
Who with the wine of the wrath because of her wantonness
Did make all the nations drunken,

and a third, who specifies the judgment to be inflicted on the worshippers of the Beast—those who have received his mark upon them. They shall, indeed, be made to drink of the wine of God's wrath, poured unmixed into His cup: "They shall be tortured with fire and brimstone in the sight of God, the holy angels, and of the Lamb. And the smoke of their torment goeth up for the ages of the ages, and they have no rest, day nor night."[1]

The little vision that follows is more than a mere blessing upon those who have conquered. It says: "Write—Blessed are *forthwith* the dead who die in the Lord! Yea, saith the Spirit; let them rest from their labours, for their works follow them." This declares that the dead have not merely to wait for the Last Coming for their reward; neither need they "labour any more". Their works accompany them into their heaven, and "from now on" are they truly blessed. Even as those who give their adoration to the world, though they live, are dead, so these, who have resisted and were slain, are immortalized, and their works along with them, and their worship; and that supreme work of worship, their death.

---

[1] We need not dwell on the misuse made, especially in the Middle Ages, of the phrase "Eternal Gospel", which it is the duty of the first of these angels to announce upon the earth. All sorts of semi-heretical interpretations were given of it. It probably just means that God's proclamation holds good for ever, though all else passes away, even the greatest of persecuting forces, like Nineveh, and Tyre, and now Rome—for the formulas "she fell", etc., are modelled on the Old Testament denunciations of those pagan powers. Is St. John's little "note", "Here is the patience [endurance] of the saints", to be joined to what precedes or to what follows? In the former case I think it will just mean that the faithful must show their endurance in putting up with the imperial persecution: in the second, that the patience finds its reward in what John is just about to say.

(c) *A Double Vision Interposed* (xiv. 14-20)

Exactly in accordance with the plan discernible in the section of the seals and in that of the trumpets, a two-parted vision is intercalated here, before the concluding vision of this section.

A white cloud; and on the cloud One seated. It is the Son of Man, Messiah, crowned, and in His hand a sickle. An angel cries to Him to strike in with His sickle, and reap, for ripe is earth's harvest. The sickle is set to work and the earth is reaped.

An angel follows; he, too, with a sickle. A voice bids him, too, cut with it the clusters of earth's vintage, for they, too, are ripe. The clusters are gathered: into the winepress outside the city are they cast, and there are trodden; blood foams forth "up to the bridles of the horses", and deluges the land to a distance of 1,600 furlongs.

Were I to think, which I do not, that John incorporated fragments from ancient apocalypses into his own, this is the passage which would most incline me to that view—though no passage could be more perfectly his own as far as diction goes. But there seems a sheer repetition—there is no hint that Christ's harvesting was not complete; that He reaped only the *good*. He spoke, indeed, Himself, of reaping wheat and tares together. And even if we are to conclude from the second part that He reaped only the good, and left the wicked to an angel, this in itself might seem strange. One might be tempted to elude this by observing that an angel *bids* the Reaper begin his work, and that *another* angel is the vintager. Is then the Reaper not really Christ? And what is this city that appears suddenly in the picture of the vintage? And what are the horses?

Let us say at once that the Reaper is certainly the

Messiah. The "other" angel means either: another, an angel; or, a fourth angel, after the three just spoken of in the first part of this vision. Nor is there room for surprise that an angel "bids" Messiah start His work. This messenger comes straight from the face of God, who alone knows the "day and the hour" that not the Son of Man Himself has knowledge of (cf. Mark iv. 29; Matt. xiii. 39, etc.); and in any case angels speak freely to God and His Christ, and we need not see in this an order, any more, I may say, than we should picture the Reaper hurling down His sickle on the earth. In Matt. x. 34 Christ says He did not come to put peace on the earth, but the Greek uses the same word, βαλεῖν. But why should Christ do one half of the work and give the rest to an inferior? Is there a certain tenderness expressed in His reserving thus the happy harvest to Himself? Or is it simply that the angels are so often associated with Himself in the picture of the Judgment? Even "the angels are the reapers" in Matt. xiii. 39, 41.

In fine, when we reflect that once the image of the winepress was well in the mind of the Seer (cf. Joel), he could scarcely forget that all executions, and in particular that of the Last Day, were conceived as taking place outside Jerusalem (Heb. xiii. 12), and very likely that the King's winepress stood, in fact, upon the Mount of Olives (Zech. xiv. 10). And the triumph of God at the Last Day was so definitely and habitually represented as a battle—the rest of the Apocalypse will show us that John most certainly held this too in his mind—and no less habitually as a treading of a winepress, that it was almost inevitable that battle-imagery should rise, as it were, across any winepress imagery, and that he who thought of the one, primarily, should find his picture shot through by secondary details belonging to the other. The winepress will, indeed, reappear in the midst of the battle-imagery in Chapter XIX.

It is fascinating to watch the interpenetrating currents, thus discernible, in an author's mind; and we are once more emancipated from supposing that John was awkwardly combining various documents, even documents that he himself might have written at different periods. There is, to me, no hint of that here.[1]

(d) A Seventh Vision (xv. 1-4)

The brief seventh vision shows the crowd of those who have crossed the Red Sea safely. They stand on that other sea, the sea of crystal before the throne—*on* it, for to the conqueror the Inaccessible offers, henceforward, His very throne to share. They hold "the harps of God", inherited from the angels who taught them their new song. That song, assuredly, not even John can write. No one can learn it till his warfare be accomplished. He puts upon his page "the song of Moses" that he sang after crossing his own Red Sea; and he speaks of the song of the Lamb, but does not, and cannot, tell us what it was. Silence followed the seventh seal, and no vision the seventh trumpet's woe; nor will John here express the ultimate union of the soul with God.

II. (i) THE SEVEN BOWLS

The first verse of Chapter XV had announced the outpouring of seven plagues upon the earth, thus "dovetailing" this group of visions into what went before, and verses 5-7 of that chapter and verse 1 of xvi compose the brief introductory vision to the actual accomplishment of this. To seven angels are given seven bowls full of the "last

[1] The imagery, we may own, is not attractive to us. The blood "up to the bridles" does not mean a spray, but a flood. Enoch i. 3 elaborates this quite disgustingly. The 1,600 furlongs mean the entire world apart from the Holy City. Moreover, the final vision necessitates this interpretation.

plagues"—last, that is, in this book which has already, at least three times related the consummation of the world—but altogether the last for that Empire towards the complete description of whose crash John is steadily advancing. Even the sounding of the trumpets was far more general in its scope. Yet we must never forget that even Rome stands only as symbol, in the long run, of the Adversary ever slain and ever renewed, throughout the world's history. When these angels appear, clouds fill the Temple of God's presence; no one can enter it; it is too late for intercession between God and His judgments.[1]

I seem to feel a certain haste in St. John's writing here; if these plagues are so important you would expect them to be written of at least at as great length as the preceding visions. And though the "pattern" into which they are grouped is that to which we are accustomed, it is but sketched, not emphasized. Is this because he is hastening on to what so clearly preoccupies him—the terrific scenes of the actual judgment upon Rome—which follow immediately? For even now he will not have said his final word. The apocalyptic visions come in successive waves, gathering in might as they advance; or, if you will, the revelation converges and converges, till, through the ever less general, it crashes on to a definitely narrowed field.

[1] We notice that it is one of the four living beings who gives the bowls that contain the plagues to the angels. John did not set out his creed in philosophical form; none the less, he did not insert his details haphazard. If it is true that the four represent—as seems more and more to be agreed—the ideal nature, we can see again how right is it to show that human nature, by its own actions, which, when wrong, work themselves out to their disastrous end, supplies to God the material in which His wrath expresses and fulfils itself. In a true sense the actions of mankind are their own judgment. In St. John's Gospel we constantly find the doctrine that men *separate themselves.* Either you "come to" and adhere to Christ, or you do not. If you separate yourself—that is your judgment. The schism is accomplished, whereas he who unites himself to God through Christ does not even move "towards judgment". In a word, man's judgment is wholly from God, and wholly from himself.

(a) *A Group of Four Plagues* (xvi. 1-9)

These new plagues of the mystical Egypt, then, begin. A group of four. A murrain upon men who have accepted the mark of the Beast. The brand gangrenes in their very flesh. The very soil is corrupted. Then the sea: it becomes blood. And then the fountains of fresh water: they, too, become blood, and the "angel of the waters" recognizes that the judgment is just—the Adversary had poured out Christian blood like water: he shall be made to drink it. And the very altar sends forth a voice with its incense-clouds, acknowledging the same. And the fourth plague smote the sun, and men were burned with its terrible heat; but like Pharaoh, they made their hearts hard.

Earth, sea, fresh waters, and the sky have thus been smitten.

(b) *Two Plagues* (10-12)

The next two plagues strike the throne of the Beast (that is, Rome; men "chew their tongues" in their agony; horrible picture! Is it lest they cry out, and confess their sin? For they are not converted from their blasphemy) and the Euphrates, so that the great river-barrier is dried up, and a road is left clear for the Eastern kings to accomplish their invasion.

(c) *A Double Vision* (13-16)

A very brief, yet double, intercalated vision, connected, as usual, with what goes just before, and with what will follow, though not for a while. From the mouths of the Dragon, the Beast, and his false prophet, issue foul spirits, like frogs—miracle-working demons—that go to all the kings of the world to summon them to the final battle.

And, thus summoned, they in fact collect together "in the place that is called in Hebrew Harmagedon".

A word on this singular conception. Verse 14 read in connection with xix. 20 would show, if need were, that the False Prophet is none other than the Second Beast. Why are these spirits "frogs"? The Egyptian plague of frogs, hitherto not utilized, would suffice to suggest the image. Add to this, that the intolerable ubiquitous croaking of frogs, to which we, unlike the East and the South, are unaccustomed, makes the picture not inappropriate. And there is a meanness, a pettiness, about the symbol that marks John's sense of the hopeless inadequacy of the Devil and his emissaries, as against God and His great herald angels. But is John hesitating between a vision of Rome, to be pitted at last against the Parthians, and to be triumphed over by them, and summoning all other kings to her aid—or, is the drying up of the Euphrates seen as the opening of a road for Parthia, no longer conceived as God's scourge upon Rome's shoulders, but as pagan, she too, and uniting with Rome against the elect? Both visions, I dare say, interplay in John's mind for a moment. But the problem lapses, and already God our Lord, to encourage His Christians at the very outset, speaks with His own mouth to say that all these preparations are idle; even so, it is as a thief in the night that He will come, and that all will be well with His own, provided they are ready.

What is Harmagedon, "the Mountain of Megiddo"? The plain of Esdraelon was where Megiddo stood, and this plain had, in Jewish history, been that beyond all others where military disasters had occurred, owing to its fatally central position on the road between north and south— Egypt and Assyria—or the two parts of the Holy Land itself. Battle after battle had been fought there—and have been fought there in later history. Especially a Jew never forgot how the Egyptian king Nechu had there over-thrown and slain Josiah (4 Kings xxiii. 29). And though Megiddo lies in a plain, yet surely John conceives of the anti-Christian forces as encamping themselves on the hills that slope down to it, while the citadel of the Lamb is Sion. The battle-shock will take place in the plain between them. And it may well be that Ezekiel (xxxviii. 8, 21, etc.), who places the final conflict, and the defeat of Gog—see Apoc. xx. 1-10—upon the mountains of Israel, was already in John's mind.

(d) The Seventh Plague (xvi. 17-21)

Into the picture of the seventh plague the imagery to follow looks strongly forward. John sums up the result of history. A voice proclaims: "It is consummated". And Babylon—that is, Rome—fell into three parts, and every city fell in ruins, and nature shook from end to end; yet even so, John repeats, the world was not converted, and he passes on to retell these happenings, both in their narrower and their quite universal sense, in the concluding sections of his book.

PART B2: A. THE TRIUMPH OF GOD AND THE DESTRUCTION OF HIS ENEMIES

Prefatory Vision (xvii. 1-2)

One of the angels who held the bowls with the plagues summons John, saying:

Come, and I will show thee the doom of the great wanton
Who is seated upon many waters,
With whom the kings of the earth did commit wantoness,
And the inhabitants of the earth were made drunk
With the wine of her wantoness.

It might be asked how this can be, since the outpouring of the bowls has destroyed Babylon. It seems to me an admirable example of John's method. The prophecy advances, not only like great waves, but in a tide. A wave has swept forward and covered a certain stretch of ground, so to speak, and now retires somewhat, only to sweep forward and farther, crashing fully this time on to that which it did but touch before.[1] The angel reshows to John the outpouring of the bowl that ruins Babylon.

(i) *A Double Preliminary Vision* (3-18)

(*a*) John is taken to the desert. There he sees a woman seated on a scarlet beast covered with blasphemous names, having seven heads and ten horns. The woman is arrayed in purple and scarlet "gilded with gold", adorned with precious stones and pearls, and holds a golden chalice full of abominations and the filthiness of her harlotry. On her forehead a name is written—a mystical name:

"Babylon the Great, mother of harlots and of the filthiness of the earth."

John stands appalled to behold her drunk with the blood of the martyrs of Jesus.

The angel says:

Why art thou appalled? I will explain to thee the mystery of the woman and the beast and its heads and its horns. The beast that thou hast seen was, and is not, but is about to ascend from the abyss and fare forth to destruction. And the inhabitants of the world, whose names are not written from the world's foundation in the Book of Life, shall go marvelling after the beast, when they see that it was, and is not, and shall be.

[1] It may be noticed that the doom of Babylon is in reality described exactly seven times—xiv. 8, xvi. 19, xvii. 16, xviii. 2, xviii. 4, xviii. 9, and xviii. 21 and the following verses.

(Here is the meaning, thou that understandest:)

The seven heads are seven mountains, whereon the woman is seated. And they are [too] seven kings: the first five are fallen; the sixth is now; the seventh is not yet come, but once come he can remain but for a brief while. And as for the beast that was and is not, why, it is an eighth, and yet it is one of the seven, and it moves forward to perdition.

The ten horns that thou hast seen are ten kings. They have not yet received their kingship, but they take their authority, as though kings, along with the beast, for an hour. They have but one mind, and as for their power and their authority they give it to the beast. These shall war with the Lamb, and the Lamb shall conquer them, because He is Lord of lords and King of kings, and with Him those that are with Him, the called and elect and faithful.

He adds:

The waters that thou hast seen, whereon the wanton sits, are peoples and crowds and nations and tongues. And the ten horns that thou hast seen, and the beast, shall hate the wanton, and shall make her desolate and naked, and shall eat her flesh, and burn her up with fire. ... And the woman that thou hast seen is the city, the great city, the one that has royal rule over the kings of the earth.

In attempting to explain this section, I wish to set forth a simple, and perhaps old-fashioned, interpretation, but also to indicate in outline another, more complicated, certainly, but, maybe, no less probable. Those who may wish to follow it out will find it almost in the form I suggest in Père Allo's book. We can begin in any case from what is certain.

John had seen that three great enemies of Christ were preparing to attack Him—the Dragon, the Beast and his prophet, and the City Rome. It is the defeat of these, in inverse order, that he now contemplates.

There is no doubt at all but that the wanton is Rome. She is seated on a beast that has seven heads, and these, St. John is told explicitly, are the seven hills of Rome. And as for the waters "on" which she is seated—as we say that a town is built "on" such and such a river—they are the chaotic elements of which her empire was compounded.[1] At an enormous cost she gave her favours to the kingdom of the known world—venal utterly, vicious utterly, self-idolatrous, the world-harlot, gilded in true prostitute fashion, clothed in scarlet and purple, and hung with the pearls for which Roman society went mad. Again like Roman prostitutes, she placarded her name, not merely on her door, but on her forehead, where the beast's mark was, and where the Lamb's name was. The world was frantic for her; she made it drunk with her wickedness, and herself was drunk with the blood of saints and martyrs. And indeed Rome, as home of the emperors, was at her worst a nightmare of lust and cruelty.

So far the only difficulty has arisen from John's using the same image to portray two things: the beast on which the woman rides stands for the emplacement of Rome; its heads are the Roman hills.[2] But the beast has already signified the imperial power, and will do so again in a moment. However, John gives us warning of this, and we may be grateful, for it shows how free he is in his use of imagery, and how floating that imagery itself may be.

John now shifts back from this use of the beast-image, which did no more than show the woman throned like Cybele on her lion-drawn chariot. The beast reverts to being frankly the imperial power, and its heads are emperors. But why is the beast able to parody thus the

[1] The phraseology is still in great part derived from the Old Testament, and especially Jer. li.

[2] "Hinc septem *dominos* videre *Colles*, et totam licet aestimare Romam'' (Martial).

Immortal God, who is, and was, and is to come, and the Lamb, that was slain, and lived once more? Why is he described as "was, and is not, and is to come"? For two reasons it seems to me that the Roman Empire may well be thus described: for not only did it seem constantly impossible that so misshapen, extravagant, and mutinous an organization should endure—assassination had become the regular death for an emperor—but in particular, after the death of Nero, the chaotic year of Galba, Otho, and Vitellius, may quite well have looked like the collapse of the Empire itself. But in the Flavian dynasty, under Vespasian, it revived. Further, if the first reckoning of emperor-heads, given below, is correct, St. John actually leaves out in his sum of emperors those three shadowy personages. And if Nero has the role which, again, I first suggest, nothing is clearer than that St. John could have thought that the whole imperial power had died in his person, only to rise again in a few months in the person of Vespasian. John, therefore, according to this interpretation, sees first the city of Rome, and then the imperial power that sustains her; and this power, especially in its character of persecuting power, seemed constantly to be on the verge of extinction, or indeed hopelessly extinguished, as when sheer chaos followed the enforced suicide of the arch-persecutor Nero; but it had revived, and was on the eve of worse cruelties, yet none the less was on its way to final ruin.

John, then, according to his custom, proceeds to descend into more accurate detail. The beast has seven heads. They are seven emperors. Five are no more, one is, one is yet to come; but, when he does, will last but a short time. Then comes an eighth, *who none the less is one of the seven*. And John particularly challenges the reader to apply his intelligence in order to realize whom he is talking about.

This seems to me to make it clear he is alluding to definite persons. Beginning with the first Emperor, you have Augustus, Tiberius, Gaius, Claudius, and Nero. These, John says, are dead. The chaotic year of Galba, Otho, and Vitellius followed—barely emperors in any sense, and probably in no sense to one living under the Flavian dynasty, of which Vespasian was the far from disreputable first. Vespasian, then, is the sixth, and was living when John wrote, unless, which is quite in keeping with apocalyptic tradition, John throws the date of his writing back somewhat, and makes what was present to him future from the standpoint of his book. Vespasian was followed by Titus, who did, in fact, reign for scarcely more than a year—a brief flash of popularity not destined to have endured had he lived. Such, then, are the seven.

Who followed Titus? Domitian. Was there a sense in which Domitian could be called the beast itself, and also "one of the seven"? Certainly. So fierce was the impression made by Nero upon the nerves of his generation that it seemed impossible to suppose that he was dead. Notice that, incredible as it may seem, the impression was one almost as much of ghastly, perverted affection as of horror and hate. Myths then circulated that he was alive somewhere—pretenders more than once rose up to claim that they were he, and one even was maintained for a while on the Euphrates by Parthia. It had, too, been prophesied that he should reign some day in Jerusalem. ... As time went by, and it was clear that Nero was dead, the myth developed, and asserted that he would come to life again, and *Nero Redux, Nero Redivivus* became catchwords. The myth poured over into Jewish books and even Christian circles; the Sibylline books are full of references to a Nero who should return—an incarnation of the devil, or Beliar, and would-be rival of God; he should come from beyond

Euphrates, and myriads should support his claim. ... And as for Domitian, well, even non-Christian Rome had nicknamed him Nero, and as late as Tertullian the comparison was natural and spontaneous.[1]

Well then, John has already told us the number of the *Beast* is the number of a *man*; a man, as it were, incarnates in himself the Beast; and that number seemed quite clearly to be Nero's name. Nero, then, is "one of the seven", and also sums up in himself the Beast. If Domitian is a second Nero, we can forthwith see how, though he is the eighth Emperor in his own person, yet, as a second Nero, he is one of the seven, and, indeed, can be regarded, he, too, as incarnating the Beast itself. And whether his persecution had already begun, or could be surmised, or was being prophesied by John, as it would have been, were this section of the Apocalypse written under Vespasian, he did, in fact, become as good a symbol as any of the anti-Christian enemy of God.

I said I would indicate briefly another system of interpretation. This is it. The number seven is here, as everywhere else in the Apocalypse, ideal. It is true that the "five" who are dead are to be regarded as real emperors, but the seven expresses the collectivity of emperors, however many they were actually to be. The eighth, then, is some future power which, though it be animated with the same spirit as the persecuting Empire, shall yet survive the Empire *as Roman Empire*—and John implies that the anti-Christian spirit does not finish with the end of any organization whatsoever, be it Rome herself. This is a very true and impressive notion. The real Beast does, at the present, he implies, work through Rome. Do not fear; Rome shall

---

[1] It may be worth recalling that a popular conviction that some idol of the imagination is not dead, but will return, is a recurrent phenomenon. We may quote Louis XVII of France, and we know how hard it was to convince England that Lord Kitchener had perished.

be destroyed. But the Beast survives Rome, and shall continue to rage—and, indeed, each time John has seemed to relate some surely final catastrophe, he adds that not even so were men converted from their blasphemies. But again, do not fear; the Beast itself shall be, in the end of time, destroyed; and finally the Dragon himself, whose servant the Beast is.[1]

The horns which Daniel saw sprouting from the fourth beast of his vision (vii. 24) were ten kings; the ten horns of the imperial Beast are almost certainly the various powers incorporated for the time being into the Roman Empire, and into which it was destined to break up. Not yet have they their independence, but they work in concert with the

[1] Père Allo, who holds this view, holds also that the emperor-heads should be calculated from Nero himself—the first frankly persecuting Emperor; the five who are dead would then be Nero, Galba and Otho, or Otho and Vitellius, Vespasian, Titus. The one who is, is Domitian. At the death of Nero, the Empire seemed to have received its death blow; but Vespasian re-established it, and this is the healing of that wound. In a brief space the Empire was to revive also in its character of persecutor of the Church—this would be its resurrection from the abyss. Given the way in which John's mind seems to work, we need not fear to suppose that his eye most certainly looks beyond the Roman Empire as such; in fact, we maintain very strongly that it does. Still, at present I prefer the system of calculating the emperor-heads that I have given first. I experience no difficulty in taking the healing of the death-wound, and the resurrection from the abyss, as two ways of stating the same thing, just as the Beast, on its side, is a symbol used for two things—Empire and Nero—and the seven heads are explicitly stated to be now hills, now emperors. To our mind, then, at one level of his attention, John sees *Nero Redivivus* in Domitian; at another, the Roman Empire ever resurgent and ever reverting to its exterminating policy; and at yet a third, the never definitive victory of Christ until the very end; ever will there be new manifestations of the same thing; and if we want a modern instance, I should quote the horrible ebullition of material force that our generation has witnessed, coupled with an idealism that is explicitly non-religious—anti-Christian socialism, undivine humanitarianism, persecuting interdenominationalism, call it what you will. The modern parallel to the Roman spirit is the wrong nationalism, coupled with the wrong internationalism, which will have none of one thing only—God authoritatively revealed in Christ, absolute over all Cæsars. Readers are free to judge how far this is realized in Communism, anti-Catholic if not definitely atheist, and incarnate in contemporary Russia, with her satellites.

Beast and war against the Lamb. But the time will come
when they shall cease to be the support of Imperial Rome,
and shall be of one mind at least in this, to break from her,
to devastate her, and to devour and burn her. And when
the hordes of barbarians did indeed do this, when Rome
Eternal, on whose very coins "Unto Eternity" was graven,
crashed beneath their onslaught, then could Augustine
emancipate the vision from the symbols of *one* time or
place, and see nothing but God's City, *Civitas Dei*, with
the world set over against her in a struggle immortal till
the very end. Here I have no doubt but that John's conscious intention in making the Beast itself turn against
Rome is to forthshow the transcendent battle of those two
spiritual cities, incarnating itself age by age in some new
pair of combatants. In all times the Beast, seemingly slain,
should reappear, should have its *parousia*, till it perished
before the Lamb it parodied.

But, first, he hymns the doom of Rome.

(a) *A Group of Four Visions* (xviii. 1-xix. 10)
The Doom of Rome

From heaven there descends an angel of great power,
and the earth is illumined by his presence. And in a loud
voice he cries:

> She fell! she fell!—Babylon the great,
>   And she is become
> A haunt of devils and a stronghold of every unclean spirit,
>   And a stronghold of every unclean and loathly bird,
>   Because of the wine of the wrath for her wantonness
>   She gave all the nations to drink.
> And the kings of the earth committed wantonness with her,
>   And the merchants of the earth from the might of her
>   luxury grew rich.
>   Come out of her, my people,

That ye be not fellow-sharers in her sins,
And that of her plagues ye may receive nothing;
For her sins are welded together high as heaven,
And God did remember her wickednesses.
Repay her even as she has given,
Yea, pay twice and twofold according to her works.
In the cup wherein she mixed,
Mix for her double.
All her self-glorifying and her wantoning—
Even so much give unto her of torture and lamentation.
For in her heart she saith,
I sit a queen,
I am no widow, and never shall I see woe.
For *that*,
In a single day shall come her plagues,
Dearth, and woe, and death.
And with fire shall she be burnt up.
For strong is the hand of God, who did judge her.

The Dirge of Rome

And there shall weep and beat their breasts over her
The kings of the earth who committed wantoness and
luxuriated with her,
When they see the smoke of her burning,
Standing afar off, for fear of her torment, saying:
Woe, the city, the great city,
Babylon, the strong city,
For in a single hour hath come thy judgment.
And the merchants of the earth shall weep and lament
over her,
Because their merchandise no man buyeth more,
Merchandise of gold and silver and precious stone and
pearls,
And fine linen and purple and silk and scarlet,
And every scented wood and every vessel of ivory,
And every vessel of most precious wood and bronze and
iron and alabaster,

Cinnamum and balsam and incense and myrrh and
frankincense,
And wine and oil and fine flour and wheat,
And cattle and sheep and horses and carriages and slaves—
And souls of men.
The ripe fruit for which thy soul lusted is gone from thee,
And all thy lovely and lustrous things have perished from
thee,
And never more at all shall men find them.
The merchants of these things, who grew rich off her,
Shall take their stand afar off from fear of her tormenting,
Weeping and lamenting and saying:
Woe, woe, the great city,
The arrayed in fine linen and purple and scarlet,
The gilded with gold, the decked with precious stone and
pearl,
In a single hour hath this vast wealth been laid waste.
And all ship-masters, and all who sail to any port,
And sailors and all who do business upon the sea,
Stood afar off when they saw the smoke of her burning,
saying:
Who is like to the great city?
And they cast dust upon their heads, weeping and wailing
and saying:
Woe, woe, the city, the great city,
By which all who had the ships upon the sea waxed rich
out of her costliness,
For in a single hour she is made desolate.
Exult over her, O heaven,
And you saints and apostles and prophets,
For God has judged your cause against her.

The Destruction of Rome

And a strong angel took up a stone great as a mill-stone,
And he cast it into the sea, saying,
With even such a crash shall be cast down Babylon, the
great city,

And shall be no more found at all.
And the sound of harpists and minstrels and flute-players
and trumpeters
Shall be heard in thee no more at all,
And no craftsman of any craft shall be found more in thee
at all,
And sound of millstone shall be heard in thee no more at all,
And light of lamp shall shine in thee no more at all,
And the voice of bridegroom and of bride shall be heard
in thee no more at all,
Because thy merchantmen were the great men of the earth,
Because by thy sorcery all the nations were set astray,
And in her was found the spilt blood of prophets and of
saints
And of all that were slaughtered on the earth.

The Exultation of the Saints

After this the voice of the great throng in heaven
hymns the just judgment of God upon Babylon, and the
vindication of His saints. And with the angels, nature and
Church reiterate their Alleluia.

And a voice from the throne bids all, great and small,
praise God, for He has established His reign.

"And to Him will we give the glory, for the marriage of
the Lamb is come, and His bride hath made herself ready.
And it hath been given her to robe herself in linen white and
shining, and the linen is the righteous actions of the saints."

And blessed were they who were called to the marriage
feast of the Lamb.

(b) A Group of Two Visions (xix. 11-21)

The sections relating the downfall of the Beast and of the
Dragon are remarkably short compared with what St.
John has said about the crash of Rome; on the other hand,

they are clear, except for one point. Perhaps, too, the imagery is less impressive, less attractive, certainly, to modern taste. But it must be recalled, first, that the phraseology is, here especially, traditional, being very closely connected with Ezekiel, as was the dirge, and that it is explicitly stated to be symbolical. The sword with which Christ will slay His enemies is His word, and the birds that will eat their flesh are no more material than that word is.

Heaven opens: a white horse, and He who is seated thereon is called faithful and truthful, and in justice He makes His war, and is Judge. His eyes are like fire, His sword is the word of His mouth; He wears many crowns of conquest; His hand holds the Messianic shepherd's iron-shod club; upon His mantle and His thigh is inscribed: King of kings and Lord of lords.[1] His name, John tells us, is The Word of God—and yet, no one knoweth His name save Himself. Even that name, the Word, on which John will dwell so solemnly in his Gospel, is but a *name*. That which it stands for—the Self, the Essence of the Word, being God, none save God can comprehend.

And the birds of the air are summoned to feast off the flesh of those slain in the final battle against God's enemies. And though all the world was counter-called to take part in that battle, the Beast and his false prophet were captured, and alive they were cast into the lake of fire, burning with brimstone. And the rest were slain with the sword.

Now if indeed the Beast is—and without doubt he is—something more generic than the Roman Imperial power, something of which that power was no more than an expression, an incarnation, if you will—then is it not

---

[1] Perhaps on His belt? Or, was John thinking of equestrian statues, which sometimes had the name of their original graven on the thigh, where the folds of the cloak lay even?

strange that the Second Beast, the False Prophet, accompanies him into this realm of the Last Days? Surely the special Asiatic persecution could not be conceived as something wider than itself, however universal the Beast might be? Unwilling to think that John simply "threw in", as it were, this symbol here too, and lest a reader might be tempted to ask, What became of the False Prophet? We answer by suggesting that he *did* stand for something that was just beginning to exist in St. John's day—the philosophic universalism, or religious syncretism (fusion) in its later form, which, with no airs of persecution, but with sweetly reasonable arguments, gave the world to understand that all religions, all cults, were true and right, standing as they did for no more than symbol of the deepest thing of all—the inaccessible Truth. This vague all-embracing theosophy, which used for its symbol the sun, was indeed the closest ally imperial autocracy ever had, and was the last great effort of paganism against Christianity, and far more consciously so than any separate religion or superstition was in St. John's day.

Such a tendency, moreover, is indeed permanent, and never has it been more noticeable than now. As I said, the anti-Christian force of today is not this cult or that, but materialism (which can express itself in many ways besides the sword—there are districts where it is indeed impossible to "buy or sell" unless you are a Freemason) and a diffused, semi-mystical, semi-philanthropic universalism, which tolerates all, in creed or behaviour, save him who says: One thing is true—one way is right. And that, the Christian, and he alone, declares; and of Christians, the Catholic alone can adequately say so.

The other point is this. That with which Christ exterminates His foes, is His Word. But, St. John insists, His Word is Himself. He is the Word. Here is the whole doctrine

of the Fourth Gospel, that John was yet to write. By
the mere fact of Christ's coming, those who are His are
separated from those who are not. Men "come" to Him,
or, if they love the dark, forthwith separate themselves,
and pronounce thereby their own judgment. He who
refuses to believe is already "in a state of judgment", of
condemnation, and, should he persist, "his sin remaineth".
In his isolation he perishes. Into such depths of spiritual
truth does this scene, that some might find harsh and
material, invite us to look.

(c) *A Double Vision* (xx. 1-10)

The defeat of the Dragon itself is told at scarcely
greater length, but the passage provides us with perhaps
the most discussed problem of the Apocalypse.

An angel descends from heaven, holding the key of the
abyss, and a great chain. He seizes the Dragon—the
primeval serpent, the Devil, Satan—and binds him for a
thousand years. He seals him into the abyss for those
years, and thereafter he shall come forth again, though but
for a brief space. Forthwith, a vision of thrones—"and
men sat down thereon—yea, the souls of those who had
been beheaded for the witnessing to Jesus and the word of
God, and all those who had not adored the Beast, nor his
image", nor been marked with his mark. "They lived and
they reigned with Christ for a thousand years. The rest of
the dead did not live till the thousand years were over.
This is the first resurrection. Happy and holy are those who
have their share in the first resurrection. Over them the
second death has no power, but they shall be kings and
priests of God, and shall reign with Him, the thousand
years."

Once those years are over, Satan shall be unbound and

come forth to set once more the nations astray—the nations of the world's four corners—Gog and Magog shall collect them from all over the surface of the earth, and besiege the camp of the saints and the beloved City. But fire from heaven devoured them, and the Devil himself was thrown into the lake of fire and brimstone where are the Beast and the False Prophet, and there they shall suffer torments for ever and ever.

I would suggest, first, that since the defeat of the Beast, as summing up all the anti-Christian forces in the world, is certainly to take place at the end of time, so must that of the Dragon. They synchronize. Therefore these visions, the "thousand years" included, not only need not, but cannot, be conceived as showing things that happened after the defeat of the Beast. Therefore, the "millennium" exists while ordinary history is proceeding, and comes to an end only when history itself shall close with the triumph of God over all His enemies alike.

I see, then, that John relates, in succession, the contents of three levels of perspective, though the happenings on each several level are simultaneous, or, at least, the content of the deepest layer coincides with the successive masses of events which compose the second level, and the second level itself is, as it were, tied down to time and space upon the first level. Let me explain that. Here are the Christians being persecuted by an emperor. That is an event proper to one age and one place—the Rome of Nero and Domitian. But John sees further than this, just a little further to begin with. He sees a collectivity of emperors—the persecuting Empire—the Beast. This deepens the perspective so slightly that we can still call it the first level, for it is still concerned with Imperial Rome as such. But then, John sees further still—much further. He sees that never in the world's history will there not be such a Beast—smitten to death he revives and renews his attack. Only with the end of the world itself will that Beast come to his own end. But deeper still than universal history does John see. We might say the Apocalypse is more than a philosophy of history, even religious. He looks right down into the roots of evil—spiritual evil—the ultimate Adversary. That is Satan. John sees his overthrow no less than that of his instruments, and that then God shall be "All in all".

But meanwhile he is "bound for a thousand years". What does that mean? We follow the interpretation that has won to itself all Catholic thought, I understand, since Augustine, and much other opinion, even independent.

John gives here the whole history of Satan since the coming of Christ. That was his defeat, his enchainment. His chance of setting the world astray is enormously diminished. The Church already reigns, the whole Church, not only the blessed dead, but the living, too, who are faithful; they sit with Christ and judge; with them is truth and the law of right. The reign and the judgment are spiritual—there is no hint that this relative triumph of the Church is comparable to the Empire that has been seen to fall—indeed, it may be expected to be as unlike it as Lamb is unlike Dragon. None the less, this period of grace for all and glory for some is the first resurrection, and to those who persevere there remains no future disaster. The second resurrection, when the rest of the dead live again, those, that is, who have lived the earthly, but not the heavenly life, will be brought about only at the end of the Christian dispensation, and they "rise to condemnation".

That dispensation will close with a renewed but brief effort on the part of evil—but that, too, shall end in defeat. Gog and Magog—I need not go into detail as to the historical sources of this symbol by which Ezekiel first portrayed the final conflict, for that is what they stand for

—sum up the final onslaught of the world upon God's beloved City, the Church. In a word. There are not two second comings of Our Lord. But the reign of the saints does not begin independently of His coming. Therefore, the period of the Incarnation, of grace in the world, is that of the "millennium", and it will end with the Second Coming and not before; and this period of bliss is one of spiritual bliss, and perfectly consistent with all the tribulations that the Apocalypse has described, not one of which can reach or injure the perfect peace of the Christian's soul.

(d) A Seventh Vision (11-15)

Forthwith after this, John, in a brief vision, displays to us the final Judgment—a sort of synopsis of, and seal upon, all that has passed.

Again a throne—a great white throne, and before the face of Him who sat thereon "heaven and earth fled away and there was no more place found for them". The dead, great and small, stood up before the throne; the sea gave up the dead that were in it; and death and Hades gave up the dead that were in them; and all were judged from the outspread books according to their deeds.

And death and Hades were cast into the lake of fire— and this is the second death. A final death. For death itself was plunged therein, and had no more power among men. There are left those, precisely, whose names are written in the Book that is "of Life".

THE DOUBLE CONCLUDING VISION OF THE NEW JERUSALEM (xxi. 1-xxii. 5)

In the account of the New Jerusalem that will follow, two points have interfered with the serenity of commentators. One is merely pictorial. St. John seems, in verse 16, to describe the City as a gigantic cube. Its breadth, length, and height are each 12,000 stades, practically miles. In any case, the numbers are, of course, "ideal" and must not be visualized too exactly. But how can one visualize at all a cubic city? How is one to place rivers, trees, and the like in any such strange mass? And the surrounding wall, which is particularly described as "high", and yet was but 144 cubits, rather over 200 ft. high, would have looked as nothing compared to the vast block it encircled. Though I am inclined to think that in these measurements St. John was not intending you to see the City in imagination at all, yet in all his other details he so forces you to contemplate it that a modern reader at least may be grateful for any help to minimize his visual difficulty. It is surely clear that St. John sees the City, not as a cube (which he does not exactly say), but as a pyramid in shape—in fact, that the New Jerusalem, as it descends from heaven, as it were clothes the great mountain peak on which it settles. Within the tall circuit of its rampart the holy mountain rises, terrace above terrace, slope beyond slope, clad in the soft radiance of the pearl, and the transparent gold and the incandescent loveliness of its jewels. High on its dazzling summit the throne of God and of the Lamb is set, and from the throne goes leaping the River, cascading down the sides of the great mountain through the groves of the Tree of Life. Let that then, if we will, be our "composition of place" for this concluding chapter.

The other point is more serious. It is urged that John does not say plainly whether this New Jerusalem is on earth, or heavenly; whether the consummation has, indeed, been reached, or whether there is work yet to be done. For, how shall the "heathen"—the "peoples"—walk in its light if the world is quite converted? *Whence* shall "kings" come to her? (verse 24).

Let us as quickly as may be rid ourselves of these chill misconceptions. John's traditional and consecrated phrases have not for point that there still are kings and peoples, but, that they *do* come; that it is in the light of God that they walk—"In Thy light shall we see light", and "All the world has gone after" her. And, in so far as there is still an "earth", it is a new earth. All the former things have gone by. There is no more sea to separate. And, if at all John's eye turns back towards the horrible contrast of what was, it sees that those who went of old to the wicked city that has perished now come to the perfect and pure Jerusalem, the Bride.

Deeper than this, surely, is the truth that John here, as in his Gospel, makes no *absolute* break between the new and the old. "Glory is grace at home." And his vision of the Church does not cleave her history in two. Already those in whom grace and the new life are, are wedded to Christ. He shows here the manifestation and eternalization of the thing that we are, albeit still precariously. Already we are the Body of Christ, though still we can "die out" of it. Already we are His Bride, though, alas! we may still pronounce our own divorce. God's city is both now and hereafter; it is both visible and invisible, both a prize and a gift; truly in us men, and "from heaven".

It remains only to say that, for a Jewish writer, the rapid transitions from the metaphor of a city to that of a bride afforded no difficulty. So had Sion immemorially been thought of.[1]

> I saw a new heaven and a new earth, for the first heaven and the first earth have passed away, and there was no more sea. And the holy city, the New Jerusalem, I saw coming down from heaven, from God, prepared as a bride that has

[1] In one apocalyptist the City turns, before his very eyes, into the Bride. John shuns this metamorphosis.

made her ready for her bridegroom. And I heard a great
voice, saying:

Behold, the tabernacle of God with men!
And He shall tabernacle with them, and they shall be His
people,
And He shall be: GOD WITH THEM.
And He shall wipe away every tear from their eyes,
And death shall be no more,
And mourning and crying and pain shall be no more.
For the former things have passed away.

The marriage harmony of all that is has been completed,
the sea of separation is gone for ever, and God lives in the
men He made, and they in Him.

And He that was seated upon the throne did say:
Behold, I make all things new.
And He said:
Write, for these words are faithful and true.
And He said to me:
It has come to pass.
I am the Alpha and the Omega,
The Beginning and the End.
I, to him that thirsteth, will give from the source of the
water of life,

A free gift.
These things shall the conqueror inherit,
And I will be to him his GOD, and he shall be to Me a son.
But as for the cowards and the unbelievers and the defiled
and the murderers and the wanton and the sorcerers and
the idolaters and all liars—their share is in the pool burning
with fire and brimstone, which is the second death.

Are we then taught the profound lesson that in the very
suffering and the punishment, God's mercy and goodwill
triumph, by the fact that it is one of the angels who held
the seven plagues who now summons John? He says:

Come, and I will show thee the Bride, the Spouse of the Lamb. And he took me away in spirit unto a mountain great and high, and he showed me the city, the holy city, Jerusalem, descending from heaven, having the glory of God.

Her radiance is like a most precious stone, like a jasper stone like crystal.

A high wall is round her to protect her, and at each of its twelve gates stands its angel-sentinel, and on the gates all the names of the twelve tribes of God's Israel, and the foundations are the twelve Apostles of the Lamb. The foundations are a rainbow glow of jewels—the soft green of the jasper, the deep blue-green of lapis-lazuli; chalcedony, green, the ancients tell us, like the peacock's tail or the shifting colours of a pigeon's throat; then emerald; then sardonyx, in which white mingles with transparent rose; in the sardian stone, the rose deepens to crimson, and the chrysolite, the beryl, and the topaz reintroduce the softest yellows and golden greens, till in the sapphire and the amethyst the glorious blue melts into violet. And the gates are pearls, and the City rises through green of jasper and refulgent yet translucent gold to its summit.

And there? The Source of its radiance: the Light no more inaccessible, but pervasive through the whole.

A temple saw I not therein,
For the Lord, God, the All-Governor, is her Temple,
And the Lamb.
Yea, the city hath no need of the sun nor of the moon,
That they should give her light,
For the glory of the Lord did give her light,
And her lamp is the Lamb.
And the nations shall go to and fro in her light,
And the kings of the earth carry their glory into her.
And her gates shall never be shut by day—
As for night there is none in her.

And they shall bring into her glory and the honour of the
  nations.
And never shall there enter into her anything unclean, or
  that maketh defilement or a lie,
But only those that have been written in the Book of Life
  of the Lamb.

Then the angel shows to John a river of water of life,
brilliant like crystal, proceeding from the throne of God
and of the Lamb. And as it flows through the wide places
of the City, on either side of it spring up the woods of the
Tree of Life, continually bearing its fruit, and its very
leaves are for the healing of the nations. It is the Holy
Spirit, fully given at last, and the rush of that river makes
glad the City of God, and its spray, refreshingly falling
upon all hearts, sinks into, impenetrates and indwells
them, to rise thence once more in the flooding fountain of
the charity of Christ (John vii. 37-9).

> And no thing that is accursed shall exist more, but the
> throne of God and of the Lamb shall be in her, and His
> servants shall serve Him, and shall behold His face, and His
> name is on their foreheads. And night shall be no more, nor
> have they need of light of lamp nor light of sun, for God shall
> shed light upon them, and they shall reign to the ages of the
> ages.

THE EPILOGUE

JOHN seeks to end his book. But through the human voice divine and angelic voices keep breaking—the seer finds it hard quite to return from ecstasy to earth.

And he said to me: These words are faithful and true, and the Lord, the God of the spirits of the prophets, hath sent His angel to show to His servants what must happen swiftly.

And lo! I am coming swiftly. Blessed is he that keepeth the words of the prophecy of the Book of Life, this book.

And it was I, John, who heard and saw these things! And when I had heard and seen, I fell and bowed down before the feet of the angel who showed these things to me. And he said to me: No, do it not. I am a fellow-servant of thine and of thy brothers the prophets and of those who keep the words of this book. Bow down to God.

Then He said to me: Seal not up the words of the prophecy of this book. For the moment is at hand. Let sinners sin yet more, and the foul be fouler still—and let the righteous do yet more righteous works and the holy sanctify him still— lo! I am coming quickly, and My reward with Me, to render unto each according to his work. I am the Alpha and the Omega, the First and the Last, the Origin and End.

Happy are they who wash their robes that they may have right to the Tree of Life, and that by the doors they may enter into the City. Outside—the dogs and the sorcerers and the impure and the murderers and the idolators and all who love and act a lie.

I, Jesus, have sent My angel to witness to you these things concerning the Churches.

I am the Root and the Race of David, the bright and morning Star.

> And the Spirit and the Bride say: Come!
> And let him who is athirst come.

Let him who wills take of the water of life, a free gift.

I bear witness, I, to whomsoever hears the words of the prophecy of this book.

If anyone adds to them, God shall add to him the plagues that are written in this book:

And if anyone takes away from the words of the prophecy of this book, God shall take away from him his share from the Book of Life, and from the Holy City, that have been told of in this book.

> He who bears witness to these things saith:
> Behold, I come quickly.

> Even so; Come, Lord Jesus.

The grace of the Lord Jesus be with all.   Amen.

With these broken sentences the Apocalypse concludes. Do you not veritably feel the frail human creature still shaken, beaten to and fro, by the Spirit, with the irresistible voice still crying or whispering through him its last few words, and how the heavenly light is still pulsing within his flame?

It is on this weaker side, his human servanthood, that we may least fear for a moment more to contemplate St. John.

His book has been called "inhuman". He, at any rate, is not that, with his eyes wide open, surely, to the beauty of every colour, and the transfiguration of sea and sky by light. Nor to the multiplicity of things that filled his world: his alertness to all the imagery of paganism, Judaism, "civilization", that was overlaid on nature, and his catching of it all up into the Christian vision that transfigured it too, gave it its true meaning and fulfilment, and thus sanctified it. Even when his duty is denunciation you may know that he had watched—with admiration in his very horror—how the gorgeous merchandise pouring from the Orient to Rome held every beauty of opulence that should make magic for the eye. And you cannot but surmise a certain fascinated horror even in his contemplation of the city Rome, the world-wanton.

But how fresh you feel him, how free, when he can rise from that charged atmosphere of flamboyant corruption into the clear world where all is golden and white, where the mad music of the Asiatic mountains or of Roman banquet rooms is left behind, and he is plunged in the great hymn of nature unblemished and of heaven, and he can listen to the universal Sanctus, like the "voice of many waters", pure and tremendous and calm. But of those visions in a moment.

You are caught up, too, by him into a great sense of consecrated history; and you are grateful that, in spite of all, he has not forgotten his own folk, but is so penetrated with the very rhythm and immemorial phrasing of the Old Testament. That, too, he lifts up and implants into the New, so that you feel, by a strange paradox, that the Old is the echo of the New, and that Christ's voice has sung itself back into the ages, and that all through the manifold half-articulate outcry of those generations the answer of the destined Son of David was ever to be heard. Prophet and Patriarch were not one of them for nothing; nothing is frustrated or discarded. If the Apostles are the foundations of the completed City, the sons of Israel are its gates; and the desire for Christ, with which those ages travailed, has passed almost without shock into the joy that the Son has indeed been born into the world. God has not made refuse of His ancient work; He has not turned His back upon the history of half the centuries.

For my part, I shall never regret the imagery St. John derived from his ancestors. I shall never feel inappropriate or out of date the scorpion-locusts, the spirits hoarsely, restlessly croaking their way through the world like frogs. Still less, of course, the terrible horsemen, the angelic trumpeters, the strong eagle-angels of God, who do not fear to contemplate that Sun; nor the holy hill, nor those rivals, Dragon and Beast and Lamb, Mother and Bride and Wanton. But what of the "Last Day" imagery, and, still more anxious, the scenes of blood and war? Well, those fallen stars, the heavens shrivelled like a burning scroll, are embedded in the language that Our Lord used; and over it He spreads His lovableness, and the words, because they are His too, have become what else they might not be. And as for the Horseman who rides forth with His raiment dyed in blood, and who makes pitiless war on evil, and destroys it, I seek to welcome it because it leaves no excuse for palliations, for complaisant slackening off of our hatred and terror of sin.

For it is sin that is destroyed, not the soul, even sinful, that is hated. Even when St. John sees a City, a system—a philosophy, we should say today—that "sets the nations wandering", that denies the only Way and plunges through marshes after will-o'-the-wisps, and leads men forth to perish in the desert, where for *them* there is no "place prepared", where, for them, there will fall no bread from heaven, it is still the system that he loathes, the lie-in-the-soul that it preaches and imposes; the very Cæsars, had he met them, he would have pleaded with in the charity of Christ. But on sin there can be no warfare made too fierce; and the Lamb Himself turns His gentleness and humility to wrath and invincible indignation, and the Word of His mouth becomes a sword, no other sword so keen.

This lesson, if none other, is cried aloud by the Apocalypse—that the world does not offer us nonchalantly a choice between good and the less good, even between good and ill, but that there is a conflict, an appalling battle for our souls; that the armies of heaven and hell are clashing over us and for us; that Dragon and Wild Beast are ravening for us; that Satan has no will but to brand us forever with his mark; that if we do not worship God, and find Him everywhere and re-worship Him there again, the whole world turns into an idol, into a thousand idols; and what should be for us an image and a likeness of God, without interspace becomes the image of the Beast. John is maddened, one might almost dare to say, by the sight of men involved in these tremendous things, and knowing it not.

Perhaps that is some reason for the sudden fierce loathing expressed in the condemnation of the Laodicean Church. It is not merely a paradox when we read: "I would that thou *wert* hot or cold." Even a wrong extreme is, we often find, more promising than the merely neutral. John feels, that if you do not love Our Lord, you ought, at least, to hate Him; if you hate, you *can* love; but there are those who are unable, apparently, to take any due attitude towards Him. To be in contact, as we necessarily are, with these vast realities, and to be unaware of them—that is the fatal state. How well John would have understood, we feel, those who persecute the Church; how appalled by the spectacle of a race or generation that was obtuse to the point of not realizing that there was anything there worth minding about—unable to catch even one ray from the celestial vision.

Not like that was the world he looked out upon, nor

even the world as in the main it ever should become. Even a country out of which the very memory of the supernatural has been smitten still feels at times that in the Church it is confronting a unique mystery—a thing quite outside its ordinary understanding—and *that* it hates. Well, better hate and hurt than just ignore. You can never grow to love what you do not even see.

But John's world had been challenged by the Church, and by no means ignored the challenge.

Therefore he could look first, or nearest, on that world and harbour no illusion about quite the most material of its contents—whether round about his home in Asia, or over the horizon where Rome lay. No wonder, then, that his prophecy, in the first wave of its on-sweeping tide, crashes full on to the harlot-city and tells its doom. He knows she will not last: what city does? What empire? Tyre had gone, and Nineveh, and Egypt was but the ghost of her old self, and after what to him was no long time should sleep under her sands. And even before that, Rome would have fallen and contain no more Cæsars. But not for that would the Beast who ruled her now give up his tyranny. Glutted with her flesh, when he should have stripped her bones naked, when in the person of her dynasties he should seem himself to have been made an end of, that hideous travesty of the Lamb should rise once more in rivalry and in a thousand forms of Cæsarism should claim the things that were God's and rage against the faithful of those yet distant ages who should refuse them. This sinister throb in history, these fleeting triumphs of God's saints in the outward world, would ever be succeeded by the rising and re-rising of the Beast and his false prophets, the alternate cursing and cajoling that the faithful must experience—that is what the prophet sees and of what he warns us.

Still deeper, he sees no more even the great systems, tendencies, moods of a godless world, but the ultimate forces at their battle—the Dragon and the Lamb. True, within the triumph which the Cross and Resurrection most necessarily are, Satan is bound even now, and his powers to set nations erring are in check. But not for that is his malice stayed. Should God allow, he will come forth again, raging the more horribly because his time is short, and when his time is over, then shàll the victory be consummated and he forbidden any more to rage. When that shall be, of that day and hour, and of the manner of its coming and being, we most assuredly have no knowledge. But we have our promise and our sanction. It remains for us only to be found among the sealed.

No one can fail to experience the profound sense of awe that broods upon John's Apocalypse. Not only is it felt in those sudden refusals to speak—that shrinking from any image whatsoever—as when there is silence in heaven, or when the seventh trumpet brings with it no vision, or when, for the New Song, he substitutes the ancient hymn of Moses. But it exists, surely, throughout the first great vision of the eternal Christ, moving in His Churches, and more than ever in the grave vision of the throne whereon the Unnamed has His seat. That vision, I said, remains as calm, unaltered background during all the rest. No ripple disturbs the glassy sea; none of the earthly conflict reaches it.

But I would note that, even so, not once does John represent God without the nature He created. Not only "ten thousand times ten thousand, thousands of thousands" of spirits do Him ceaseless liturgy, but the race of men, as seen in God's plan, is there, and all that nature that He, on creating it, pronounced to be so good, is to this side and that, and before, and behind Him. All join in the eternal Sanctus of His praise. Through the long Mass of history, the Agnus, it is true, is humbly cried by those martyr-priests who offer their own lives along with His; but, at the end, albeit the visions sweep full circle, and come back to that throne and the eternal now of heaven, nature redeemed, triumphantly made super-nature, immortalized, divinized, is still there, with one voice uttering its "Gloria Patri, et Filio, et Spiritui Sancto". The world has become the Church; Jerusalem, descending from on high, has clothed the mountain that is all the earth, has absorbed sun and moon and stars, is Catholic, Apostolic, Holy; in her are wedded the Origin and the End—all the letters have united themselves, now, into the one Word. At last all things are made new—new song, new name, new Jerusalem, new heaven and earth. Not by annihilation of the old, but by taking it all up, at last, into the divine union.

On such a vision does John's eye rest before the heaven of Apocalypse closes above him. And from it he returns to a world where none the less he may find his communion, where Christ enters into the house of each faithful soul, "and I will eat with him, and he with Me". *Et Verbum caro factum est.* The door need not stay shut; at the knock of grace, please God, it opens—"Come, Lord Jesus"—and admits the patient, gentle Friend.